A Self-Study Guide for the ISTQB Foundation Exam

Certified Tester Foundation Level (CTFL) 2018 Syllabus

2nd Edition

(Updated for CTFL Syllabus 2018 V3.1)

Chhavi Raj Dosaj

ISTQB certified registered trainer for ISTQB Foundation Level (CTFL), ISTQB Foundation Level- Agile Tester Extension (CTFL-AT) & ISTQB Advanced Level- Test Manager (CTFL-ATM)

A Self-Study Guide for the ISTQB Foundation- Certified Tester Foundation Level Exam (CTFL) 2018 Syllabus

By Chhavi Raj Dosaj

Copyright © Chhavi Raj Dosaj
No part of this publication may be reproduced, stored in a retrieval system or transmitted in any form or by any means, electronic, mechanical, photocopying, recording, scanning, or otherwise without either the prior written permission of the Author or authorization through payment of the appropriate per-copy fee to the Author. For permission please contact the author.

This document also contains registered trademarks, trademarks and service marks that are owned by their respective companies or organizations. The Publisher and the author disclaim any responsibility for specifying which marks are owned by which companies or organizations.

LIMIT OF LIABILITY/DISCLAIMER OF WARRANTY: THE PUBLISHER AND THE AUTHOR MAKE NO REPRESENTATIONS OR WARRANTIES WITH RESPECT TO THE ACCURACY OR COMPLETENESS OF THE CONTENTS OF THIS WORK AND SPECIFICALLY DISCLAIM ALL WARRANTIES, INCLUDING WITHOUT LIMITATION, WARRANTIES OF FITNESS FOR A PARTICULAR PURPOSE. NO WARRANTY MAY BE CREATED OR EXTENDED BY SALES OR PROMOTIONAL MATERIALS. THE ADVICE AND STRATEGIES CONTAINED HEREIN MAY NOT BE SUITABLE FOR EVERY SITUATION. THIS WORK IS SOLD WITH THE UNDERSTANDING THAT THE PUBLISHER IS NOT ENGAGED IN RENDERING LEGAL, ACCOUNTING OR OTHER PROFESSIONAL SERVICES. IF PROFESSIONAL ASSISTANCE IS REQUIRED, THE SERVICES OF A COMPETENT PROFESSIONAL PERSON SHOULD BE SOUGHT. NEITHER THE PUBLISHER NOR THE AUTHOR SHALL BE LIABLE FOR DAMAGES ARISING HEREFROM. THE FACT THAT AN ORGANIZATION OR WEBSITE IS REFERRED TO IN THIS WORK AS A CITATION AND/OR A POTENTIAL SOURCE OF FURTHER INFORMATION DOES NOT MEAN THAT THE AUTHOR OR THE PUBLISHER ENDORSES THE INFORMATION. THE ORGANIZATION OR WEBSITE MAY PROVIDE OR MAKE THEIR OWN RECOMMENDATIONS.

Dedicated to,

My parents' Dr. Pradeep Dosaj & Mrs. Kaushal Dosaj

Contents

1. Fundamentals of Testing 3
2. Software Lifecycles 45
3. Static Testing 87
4. Test Techniques 115
5. Test Management 171
6. Tool Support for Testing 217

Acknowledgments

I would like to acknowledge that this book relies heavily on the new ISTQB Certified Tester- Foundation Level syllabus 2018 version and ISTQB standard Glossary of Terms. In some cases, certain phrases were used verbatim to ensure the content adheres to the syllabus and glossary.

I would like to thank Arun Kumar for helping me in the preparation of diagrams and Jayashree Krishnan & Smitha Srinivasan for helping me with the technical review of the book.

Trademarks

The following registered trademarks and service marks are used in this document: ISTQB® is a registered trademark of the International Software Testing Qualifications Board.

Disclaimer

Although all efforts have been made to ensure the accuracy of the contents of this book, we cannot guarantee 100% correctness of the information contained herein.

If you find any factual anomalies, grammar or spelling errors please send it along with your comments and suggestions to the author.

Overview of Exam

Introduction to Certified Tester Foundation Level

The Foundation Level qualification is aimed at anyone involved in software testing. This includes people in roles such as testers, test analysts, test engineers, test consultants, test managers, user acceptance testers, and software developers. This Foundation Level qualification is also appropriate for anyone who wants a basic understanding of software testing, such as product owners, project managers, quality managers, software development managers, business analysts, IT directors, and management consultants. Holders of the Foundation Certificate will be able to go on to higher-level software testing qualifications.

Learning Objectives

The syllabus categorizes learning objectives into three cognitive levels:

- **K1:** remember, recognize, and recall
- **K2:** understand, explain, give reasons, compare, classify and summarize
- **K3:** apply

The relevant learning objectives at K1, K2, and K3 levels are provided at the beginning of each chapter within each particular extension syllabus.

The distribution of the question based on the chapters and cognitive levels are as below:

	K1	K2	K3	Total
Chapter 1	2	6	0	8
Chapter 2	1	4	0	5
Chapter 3	1	3	1	5
Chapter 4	1	5	5	11
Chapter 5	2	5	2	9
Chapter 6	1	1	0	2
Total	8	24	8	40

Exam Structure

This exam is comprised of 40 multiple choice questions. To pass the exam, at least 65% of the questions (26 questions) must be answered correctly.

1 Fundamentals of Testing

Learning objectives for Fundamentals of Testing 4
1.1 What is testing? 5
    1.1.1 Typical Objectives of Testing 6
    1.1.2 Testing and Debugging 7
1.2 Why is testing necessary? 9
    1.2.1 Testing's contributions to success 11
    1.2.2 Quality Assurance and Testing 12
    1.2.3 Errors, Defects, and Failures 13
    1.2.4 Defects, Root Causes and Effects 14
1.3 Seven testing principles 16
1.4 Test process 21
    1.4.1 Test Process in Context 21
    1.4.2 Test Activities and Tasks 22
    1.4.3 Test Work Products 28
    1.4.4 Traceability between the Test Basis and Test Work Products 30
1.5 The psychology of testing 31
    1.5.1 Human Psychology and Testing 31
    1.5.2 Tester's and Developer's Mindsets 32
1.6 Relevant glossary terms and keywords 34
1.7 Quiz 37
1.8 Answers 40

Learning objectives for Fundamentals of Testing

This chapter provides a foundation upon which the other sections build. Following learning objectives are covered in this chapter:

1.1 What is Testing?

FL-1.1.1 (K1) Identify typical objectives of testing

FL-1.1.2 (K2) Differentiate testing from debugging

1.2 Why is Testing Necessary?

FL-1.2.1 (K2) Give examples of why testing is necessary

FL-1.2.2 (K2) Describe the relationship between testing and quality assurance and give examples of how testing contributes to higher quality

FL-1.2.3 (K2) Distinguish between error, defect, and failure

FL-1.2.4 (K2) Distinguish between the root cause of a defect and its effects

1.3 Seven Testing Principles

FL-1.3.1 (K2) Explain the seven testing principles

1.4 Test Process

FL-1.4.1 (K2) Explain the impact of context on the test process

FL-1.4.2 (K2) Describe the test activities and respective tasks within the test process

FL-1.4.3 (K2) Differentiate the work products that support the test process

FL-1.4.4 (K2) Explain the value of maintaining traceability between the test basis and test work products

1.5 The Psychology of Testing

FL-1.5.1 (K1) Identify the psychological factors that influence the success of testing

FL-1.5.2 (K2) Explain the difference between the mindset required for test activities and the mindset required for development activities

1.1 What is testing?

Software systems affect virtually every facet of life today. We use software systems throughout the day - such as awaking to an alarm set on a smartphone app, checking email and browsing internet on different devices, driving a car guided by GPS navigation system, buying groceries and other household products on e-commerce applications, using online business applications for our banking and other financial needs and the list goes on. Software systems are an integral part of our offices, hospitals, schools, and all our public transportation systems.

But many times, these software systems did not work as expected. Software systems that do not work correctly can lead to many problems, including:

- Loss of money
- Loss of time
- Brand damage
- Injury or death.

Software testing is a way to **assess the quality of the software** and to **reduce the risk of software failure** in operation.

A common misconception of testing is that it only consists of running tests i.e., executing the software and checking the results. However, test activities exist before and after test execution - activities such as planning and control, choosing test conditions, designing test cases, evaluating completion criteria, reporting on the testing progress and results, and finalizing or closure once a test phase is completed.

Some testing does involve the execution of the component or system being tested; such testing is called **dynamic testing**. Other testing does not involve the execution of the component or system being tested; such testing is called **static testing**. Static testing seeks to prevent defects by reviewing work products such as requirements, user stories, and source code.

Both dynamic testing (when the code is running) and static testing (when the code is not running) can be used as a means for achieving similar objectives (i.e. find and prevent defects) and provides information in order to improve the development and testing processes.

Another common misconception of testing is that it focuses entirely on the verification of requirements, user stories, or other specifications. While testing does involve checking whether the system meets specified requirements, it also involves validation, which is checking whether the system will meet user and other stakeholder needs in its operational environment(s).

Testing definition from ISTQB glossary- "Testing is the process consisting of all lifecycle activities, both static and dynamic, concerned with planning, preparation and evaluation of a component or system and related work products to determine that they satisfy specified requirements, to demonstrate that they are fit for purpose and to detect defects."

1.1.1 Typical Objectives of Testing

For any given project, the objectives of testing may include:

- To prevent defects by evaluating work products such as requirements, user stories, design, and code
- To verify whether all specified requirements have been fulfilled
- To check whether the test object is complete and validate if it works as the users and other stakeholders expect
- To build confidence in the level of quality of the test object
- To find defects and failures thus reducing the level of risk of inadequate software quality
- To provide sufficient information to stakeholders to allow them to make informed decisions, especially regarding the level of quality of the test object
- To comply with contractual, legal, or regulatory requirements or standards

The objectives of testing can vary, depending upon the context of the component or system being tested, the test level, and the software development lifecycle model.

For example, each test level may have a different test objective:

Test Level	Test Objective
Component testing	Find as many failures as possible and increase code coverage of tests.
Integration testing	Find as many failures as possible in the interfaces
System testing	Cause as many failures as possible so that defects in the software are identified and can be fixed
Operational testing	Assess system characteristics such as reliability or availability
Acceptance testing	The system works as expected and satisfies requirements. Provide information to stakeholders about the risk of releasing the system at a given time.
Maintenance testing	Test that no new defects have been introduced during the development of the changes

Chapter 2 provides more details about the different test levels.

Key exam take-out
There are different **OBJECTIVES** of testing: • Verify requirements • Prevent defects • Find defects and failures • Gain confidence in system • Reduce the level of risk • Providing information for decision making • Compliance

1.1.2 Testing and Debugging

Testing and debugging are different kinds of activities, both of them have an important place in the software development lifecycle.

Testing can identify errors, defects and failures. Executing tests can show failures that are caused by defects in the software. However, testing does not include correction of defects. They are reported to the developer who can fix them. Testing does, however, ensure that changes and fix are checked for their effects on other parts of the component or system.

Debugging is the development activity that identifies the cause of defects, analyze and fix such defects. Developers are responsible for debugging and any associated component testing and component integration testing required. Testers are responsible for the initial and the confirmation test. **Confirmation testing** checks whether the fixes have resolved the defects correctly in the program and the system works as intended.

Key exam take-out

- **DEBUGGING localizes** the defect, **fixes** the defect and **checks** that the fix has been applied correctly
- **TESTING confirms** that the fix **works as intended** in the system
- **Tester** is responsible for **testing** and the **developer** is responsible for **debugging** activities

1.2 Why is testing necessary?

Testing is needed because software failure can result in serious problems for the user of the software and for the organization that produces/uses the software product. Rigorous testing of components and systems, and their associated documentation, can help reduce the risk of failures occurring during operation. When defects are detected, and subsequently fixed, the quality of the components or systems is improved. In addition, software testing may also be required to meet contractual or legal requirements or industry-specific standards.

The following cases illustrate situations where software failure led to problems:

Jun 1996 Ariane 5 flight 501 software failure

On June 1996 an unmanned Ariane 5 rocket launched by the European Space Agency exploded just thirty-six seconds after its lift-off due to multiple computer failures. The rocket was on its first voyage, after a decade of a development cost of nearly $8 billion, and was carrying a $500 million satellite payload when it exploded.

Ariane 5 satellite-launching rocket reused working software from its predecessor, the Ariane 4. Unfortunately, the Ariane 5's faster engines exploited a bug that was not found in previous models. The software had tried to cram a 64-bit number into a 16-bit space. The resulting overflow conditions crashed both the primary and backup computers which were both running the exact same software.

Feb 1991 Patriot Missile software failure

A Patriot missile defense system operating at Dhahran, Saudi Arabia, during Operation Desert Storm failed to track and intercept an incoming Scud missile. This Scud subsequently hit an Army barracks, killing 28 Americans soldiers. The inquiry reported that the failure to track the Scud missile was caused by a precision problem in the software.

The Patriot system tracked its target by measuring the time it takes for radar pulses to bounce back from them. Rounding errors in the time conversions caused shifts in the system's range gate, which led to an inaccurate tracking calculation that became worse the longer the system operated. On the day of the incident, the system had been operating for more than 100 hours, and the inaccuracy was serious enough to cause the system to look in the wrong place for the incoming missile.

Apr 2008 London Heathrow Terminal 5 baggage handling system failure

During the first five days of the opening of the new Terminal 5, British Airways misplaced more than 23,000 bags, cancelled 500 flights and made losses of £16m. This all happened due to multiple failures in the baggage handling system.

On the Terminal's opening day, the system could not cope up with the vast amounts of luggage checked in and caused the entire system to become confused and shut down. It was revealed later that some "real life" scenarios which failed were not verified thoroughly enough during the testing phase.

1962 Mariner 1 flight software failure

A failure in the flight software for the Mariner 1 caused the rocket to divert from its intended path to crash back to earth. Alarmed, NASA engineers on the ground issued a self-destruct command to destroy the rocket over the Atlantic Ocean.

The investigation into the accident discovered that an incorrect formula in the software code caused the system to miscalculate the rocket's trajectory. The cost of the mission was $18 million at that time.

August 2012 Knight's Capital Group Software failure

In a single day, one of the biggest American market makers Knight capital lost a $440 million in trading. This happened due to a failure in their new trading software.

Due to the failure, the new trading software accidentally bought and sold millions of shares after the markets opened. Those trades pushed the value of many stocks up. The company's losses appear to have occurred when it had to sell the overvalued shares back into the market at a lower price.

Aug 2000- Mar 2001 Panama City radiotherapy software failure

During Aug 2000 the therapy planning software which was used to calculate shielding blocks during radiotherapy treatments was modified. The changes resulted in failures which miscalculated the proper dosage of radiation for patients undergoing radiation therapy. This was unknown to the operators and over a period of time 17 patients died and 11 were injured due to overexposure.

> **Key exam take-out**
>
> Software that does not work correctly can lead to many problems including **loss of money, time** or **business reputation** and could even cause **injuries** or **deaths**.

1.2.1 Testing's contributions to success

It is quite common for defect prone software to be delivered into operation which subsequently cause failures or otherwise not meet the stakeholders' needs.

To reduce the frequency of such problematic deliveries following is required:

- Use appropriate test techniques
- Apply these techniques with the appropriate level of test expertise
- Apply these techniques in the appropriate test levels
- Apply these techniques at the appropriate points in the software development lifecycle

Examples of these include:

- Having **testers involved in requirements reviews or user story refinement** could detect defects in these work products. The identification and removal of requirements defects reduce the risk of **incorrect or untestable features** being developed.
- Having **testers work closely with system designers** while the system is being designed can increase each party's understanding of the design and how to test it. This increased understanding can reduce the risk of **fundamental design defects** and enable tests to be identified at an early stage.
- Having **testers work closely with developers** while the code is under development can increase each party's understanding of the code and how to test it. This increased understanding can reduce the risk of **defects within the code and the tests**.
- Having **testers verify and validate the software prior to release** can detect failures that might otherwise have been missed and support the process of removing the defects that caused the failures (i.e., debugging). This increases the likelihood that the **software meets stakeholder needs and satisfies requirements**.

1.2.2 Quality Assurance and Testing

Often the phrase ***quality assurance*** (or just *QA*) is used to refer to testing but quality assurance and testing are not the same. They are related. A larger concept, quality management, ties them together. Quality management includes all activities that direct and control an organization with regard to quality.

Among other activities, quality management includes both quality assurance and quality control. Quality assurance is typically focused on adherence to proper processes, in order to provide confidence that the appropriate levels of quality will be achieved. When processes are carried out properly, the work products created by those processes are generally of higher quality, which contributes to defect prevention. For effective quality assurance root cause analysis is used to detect and remove the causes of defects. Also, findings of retrospective meetings are used to improve processes.

Quality control involves various activities, including test activities, that support the achievement of appropriate levels of quality. Test activities are part of the overall software development or maintenance process. Since quality assurance is concerned with the proper execution of the entire process, quality assurance supports proper testing.

Quality Assurance and Testing

1.2.3 Errors, Defects, and Failures

Software systems are increasingly complex, often systems are connected to many other systems. Development of these complex systems requires a great deal of time, skill and effort and during this process, **human beings can make errors or mistakes.**

These **ERRORS** can lead to the introduction of a defect (fault or bug) in the software code or in some other related work product. For example, a requirements elicitation error can lead to a requirements defect, which then results in a programming error that leads to a defect in the code.

If a **DEFECT** has been introduced into the code, then after the code is executed it could cause a **FAILURE.** If this happens then the defect has led to a failure. A failure occurs within the system.

Defects may result in failures but not in all circumstances. For example, the portion of the code where the defect exists may not be executed perhaps because some very specific inputs or preconditions are required to trigger a failure, which may occur rarely or never.

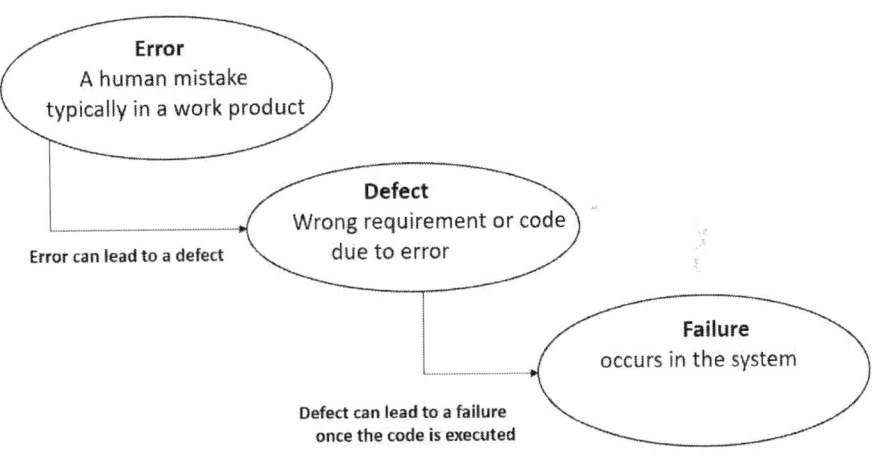

Error, defect and failure

Errors may occur due to many reasons such as:

- Time pressure makes people cut corners, and this can decrease the quality of the product developed
- Humans are not perfect; they are likely to make errors or mistakes

- Project team members are not skilled or not having relevant experience to carry on their tasks
- The complexity of the code, design, architecture
- The complexity of the underlying problem to be solved by the system
- The complexity of the infrastructure
- The complexity of the technologies or new or changing technologies
- Misunderstandings about intra-system and inter-system interfaces, especially when the interactions between them are large in number

Failures can also be caused by environmental conditions other than defects, such as:

- Radiation
- Electromagnetic fields
- Pollution
- Temperature Changes

1.2.4 Defects, Root Causes and Effects

When the tester is raising a defect, they will make an educated guess regarding what probably caused the problem. This will be the preliminary root cause value for the defect. This can be further reviewed and modified when the developer is debugging the defect. When confirming the fix, the tester will verify the root cause value entered or modified by the developer.

Typical root causes include:

- Unclear requirement
- Missing requirement
- Wrong requirement
- Code logic error
- Invalid data

The root causes of defects are the earliest actions or conditions that contributed to creating the defects. This root cause information is aggregated to determine common issues that are resulting in the creation of defects. This can help in the reduction of the occurrence of similar defects in the future. For example, if a large number of defects is caused by unclear requirements, it would make sense to apply more effort on conducting effective requirements reviews.

Root cause analysis can also lead to process improvements that prevent a significant number of future defects from being introduced.

If the defects are not found or fixed and failures are observed by the customer in the live environment. The consequences will be the **effects** of the defect.

Example:

Consider a system for the calculation of salary of the casual staff. As the calculation was quite complex business analyst misunderstood it and created wrong requirements. This resulted in a wrong code developed by the developer.

Once the system was live, it calculated the wrong salary to the casual staff. Most of the casual staff were underpaid this resulted in a number of salary-related tickets raised against finance help desk team.

In this example. Wrong requirements are the **errors**, Improper calculation of salary is a **defect,** lack of knowledge on the part of the business analyst is the **root cause** of the defect, wrong salary distribution is the **failure** and tickets raised against finance help desk team are the **effects** of the defect.

The root cause of the wrong requirement was caused due to business analysts' lack of knowledge of the salary calculation. Thus, resulting in the error while drafting the requirement. To reduce such defects in the future proper training should be provided to the business analyst for any complex salary calculations.

1.3 Seven testing principles

Over the last 50 years, there have been a number of testing principles that offer general guidelines common for all testing. The ISTQB syllabus covers seven of these principles.

Principle 1: Testing shows presence of defects, not their absence

Testing can show that defects are present, but it cannot prove that no defects are remaining. Testing reduces the probability of undiscovered defects remaining in the software but, even if no defects are found, testing is not a proof of correctness.

It may happen that during testing of the system no defects are found but the system fails during operation. This is the reason the absence of defects is not an adequate criterion for the release of the system in operation.

> **Key exam take-out**
> Even when no defects are found during testing, it can't be proved that software is defect-free.

Principle 2: Exhaustive testing is impossible

Testing everything (all combinations of inputs and preconditions) is not feasible except for trivial cases.

Consider using the exhaustive testing technique on a one-digit field of a software which accepts only upper-case alphabets. In this case the valid tests are required to check all 26 uppercase alphabets are accepted. We need to test that all invalid inputs are also rejected. Tests will be required for 0-9 digits, 26 lower case alphabet characters and 32 special charaters including space. Therefore the total of 94 test cases are required to fully test this one-digit field. If we try exhaustive testing technique for a software having 10 input fields where each input can have 5 possible values. Then just to test all the valid input values we would need 10^5 (10x10x10x10x10=100,000) test cases It is unlikely that these many test cases can be executed.

Rather than attempting to test exhaustively, risk analysis, test techniques, and priorities should be used to focus on test efforts.

Key exam take-out
• Exhaustive testing is a test approach in which all possible data combinations are used, including the implicit data combinations present in the state of the software.
• It is not possible to test all possible combinations of data input in most of the circumstances.
• This is the reason risk and priorities are used to focus on the most important tests.

Principle 3: Early testing saves time and money

To find defects early, both static and dynamic test activities should be started as early as possible in the software development lifecycle. Early testing is sometimes referred to as **shift left**. Testing early in the software development lifecycle can help prevent defects from being introduced into code. This can helps reduce or eliminate costly changes. Following diagram shows that the relative cost of fixing the defect increase with each project phase.

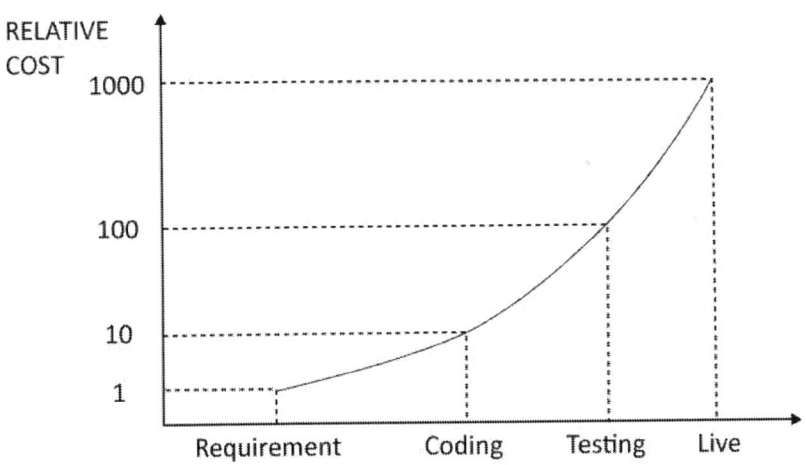

Cost of fixing defect

> **Key exam take-out**
> **Testing activities should start as early** as possible in the software life-cycle in order to find and enable the fixing of defects at the lowest cost.

Principle 4: Defects cluster together

Experience shows that, in general, a small number of software modules contain most of the defects discovered during pre-release testing or are responsible for most of the operational failures.

Therefore, the testing effort should be based proportionally on the expected and later observed defect density of modules.

The modules where the defects are clustered are often the ones bearing the highest degrees of complexity or which are difficult to understood, or which have the most degraded code (perhaps unsupported by documentation).

> **Key exam take-out**
> - 80% of the defects come from 20% of the modules (Pareto principle applied to software testing)
> - Defects are clustered in modules that are:
>   - More complex
>   - Larger
>   - More prone to changes
>   - Have been worked on by many different developers over time

Principle 5: Beware of Pesticide paradox

If the same tests are repeated over and over again, eventually these tests no longer find any new defects. This principle can be compared to the principle of getting rid of unwanted bugs from a vegetable garden. The gardener may use a pesticide to kill the bugs. Initially this may be successful; however, over time the bugs evolve and build up a resistance to the pesticide.

If those same test cases fail to find any new defects, running the same test cases, again and again, will eventually leave the tester with a false sense of security that the quality of the software is misleadingly good. If the same set of automated test cases are used for regression testing the effectiveness of these tests will decrease over time due to the pesticide paradox.

To overcome this "pesticide paradox", the test cases need to be regularly reviewed. Exisiting tests and test data may be revised. New and different tests need to be written based on different test techniques to exercise different parts of the system. All of this will help to potentially find new defects.

Key exam take-out
To overcome the pesticide paradox testing team need to: o Review test cases regularly o Add more relevant new test cases to exercise different parts of the software and remove the test cases which are not required o Assess the value of running tests in each regression run. Make sure there is a value-add from the effort

Principle 6: Testing is context dependent

Testing is done differently in different contexts. For example, safety-critical software is tested differently from e-commerce software.

Safety-critical software development is generally expected to follow a rigorous development model, where significant attention is paid to getting the requirements right and ensure error-free software as much as possible throughout the lifecycle. High level of documentation and audit trails are often mandated via industry standards.

An e-commerce software, however, is likely to be subject to on-going changes, necessitated by the changing needs of the customer. Thus, testing in this context may well take a much more agile approach with close collobration with the customer and less documentation.

> **Key exam take-out**
> - Same set of testing activities are not applicable for all applications.
> - Testing is done differently for different applications.
> - Risk can be a large factor in determining the type of testing that is needed. The higher the possibility of losses, the more we need to invest in testing the software before it is implemented.
> - Testing in an Agile project is done differently than testing in a sequential software development lifecycle project.

Principle 7: Absence-of-errors fallacy

It is a fallacy (i.e., a mistaken belief) to expect that just finding and fixing a large number of defects will ensure the success of a system.

Finding and fixing defects does not ensure that the system meets the users' expectations. For example, a software company might build a new system for a user group based on their understanding of those groups. However, thoroughly testing all specified requirements and fixing all defects found could still produce a system that is difficult to use and does not fulfill the users' needs and expectations, or that is inferior compared to other competing systems.

> **Key exam take-out**
> Finding and fixing defects does not guarantee that the system built is usable and/or fulfill the users' needs and expectations.

1.4 Test process

The most visible part of testing is the execution of the tests. However, to be effective and efficient, time should be spent on planning the tests, designing test cases, preparing for test execution and evaluating test status.

1.4.1 Test Process in Context

Contextual factors that influence the test process for an organization, include, but are not limited to:

- Software development lifecycle model and project methodologies being used
- Test levels and test types being considered
- Product and project risks
- Business domain
- Operational constraints, such as:
  o Budgets and resources
  o Timescales
  o Complexity
- Contractual and regulatory requirements
- Organizational policies and practices
- Required internal and external standards

It is very useful if the test basis (for any level or type of testing that is being considered) has measurable coverage criteria defined. The coverage criteria can act effectively as key performance indicators (KPI) to drive the activities that demonstrate achievement of software test objectives.

For example, for a mobile application, the test basis may include a list of requirements and a list of supported mobile devices. Each requirement is an element of the test basis. Each supported device is also an element of the test basis. The coverage criteria may require at least one test case for each element of the test basis. Once executed, the results of these tests tell stakeholders whether specified requirements are fulfilled and whether failures were observed on supported devices.

ISO standard (ISO/IEC/IEEE 29119-2) provides more information about test processes.

1.4.2 Test Activities and Tasks

A test process consists of the following main groups of activities:

- Test planning
- Test monitoring and control
- Test analysis
- Test design
- Test implementation
- Test execution
- Test completion

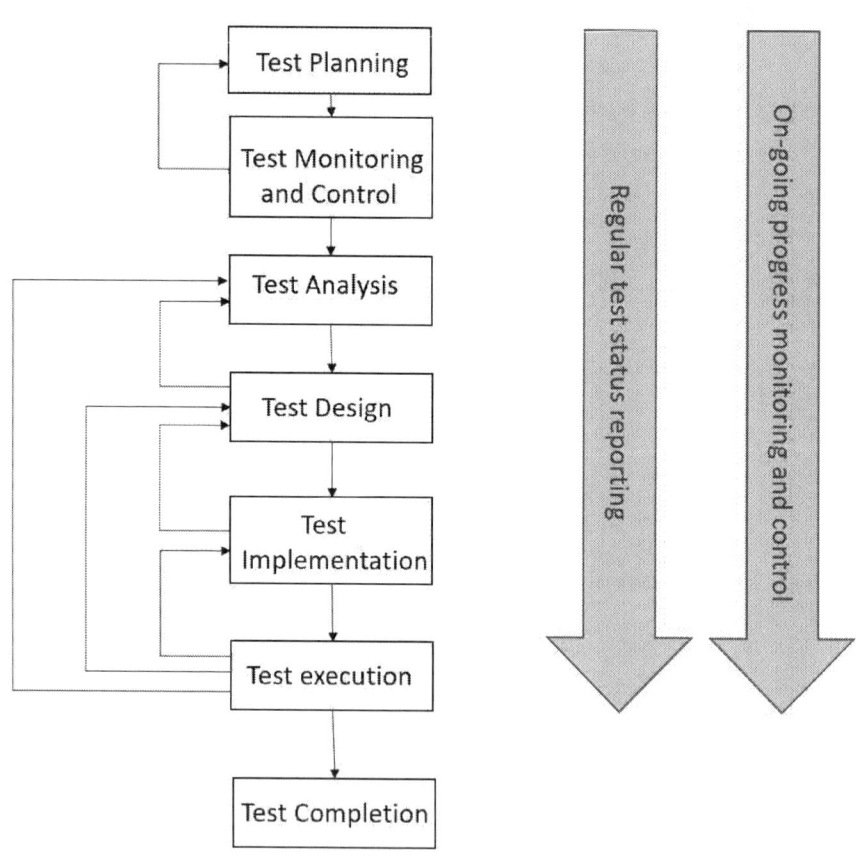

Test Process

Each group of main activities is composed of constituent activities which may consist of multiple individual tasks. These tasks would vary from one project or release to another.

Further, some of these main activity groups may appear logically sequential but they are often implemented iteratively or tailored based on the context of the system and project.

For example, Agile software development involves small iterations of software design, build, and test. Therefore, test activities also happens on a continuous iterative basis supported by on-going planning. In sequential software development, the logical sequence of main group of activities will often overlap or combined, or done concurrently, or omitted.

Test planning

Test planning is the activity of planning about the testing activities, coming up with the mission of testing, defining the objectives of testing and the specification of test activities in order to meet the objectives and mission.

Test planning has the following major tasks:

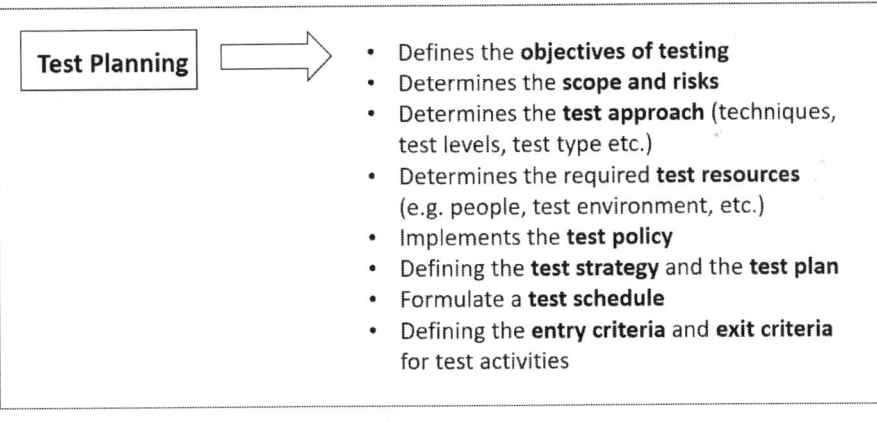

- Defines the **objectives of testing**
- Determines the **scope and risks**
- Determines the **test approach** (techniques, test levels, test type etc.)
- Determines the required **test resources** (e.g. people, test environment, etc.)
- Implements the **test policy**
- Defining the **test strategy** and the **test plan**
- Formulate a **test schedule**
- Defining the **entry criteria** and **exit criteria** for test activities

Test monitoring and control

Test monitoring and control include the **on-going activities** of **comparing actual progress against the planned progress** and reporting the status, including deviations from the plan. They involve taking actions necessary to meet the mission and objectives of the project. In order to control testing, progress should be monitored throughout the project.

Test monitoring and control have the following major tasks:

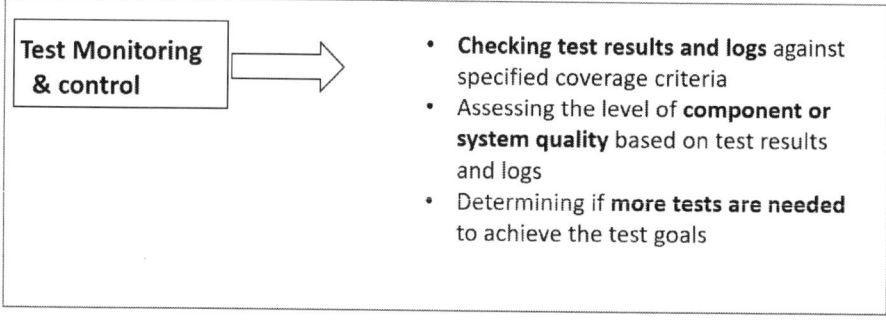

Test progress against the plan is communicated to stakeholders in test progress reports, including deviations from the plan and information to support any decision to stop testing.

Test analysis

Test analysis is the activity where general testing objectives are transformed into tangible test conditions.

It has the following major tasks:

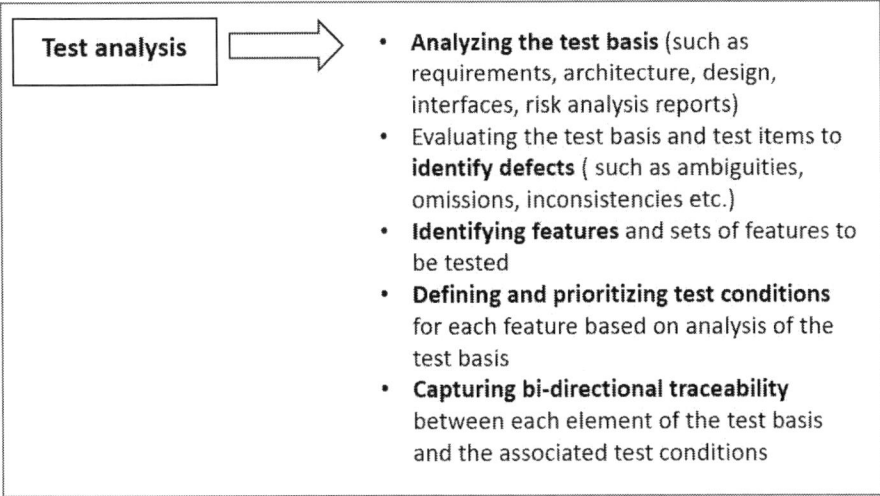

- **Analyzing the test basis** (such as requirements, architecture, design, interfaces, risk analysis reports)
- Evaluating the test basis and test items to **identify defects** (such as ambiguities, omissions, inconsistencies etc.)
- **Identifying features** and sets of features to be tested
- **Defining and prioritizing test conditions** for each feature based on analysis of the test basis
- **Capturing bi-directional traceability** between each element of the test basis and the associated test conditions

The application of black-box, white-box, and experience-based test techniques are used in the process of test analysis to reduce the likelihood of omitting important test conditions.

In some cases, test analysis produces test conditions which are to be used as test objectives in test charters. Test charters are typical work products in some types of experience-based testing.

The identification of defects during test analysis is an important potential benefit, especially where no other review process is being used and/or the test process is closely connected with the review process. Such test analysis activities not only verify whether the requirements are consistent and complete, but also validate whether the requirements properly capture customer needs.

Test design

Test design is the activity where test conditions are transformed into high-level test cases.

It has the following major tasks:

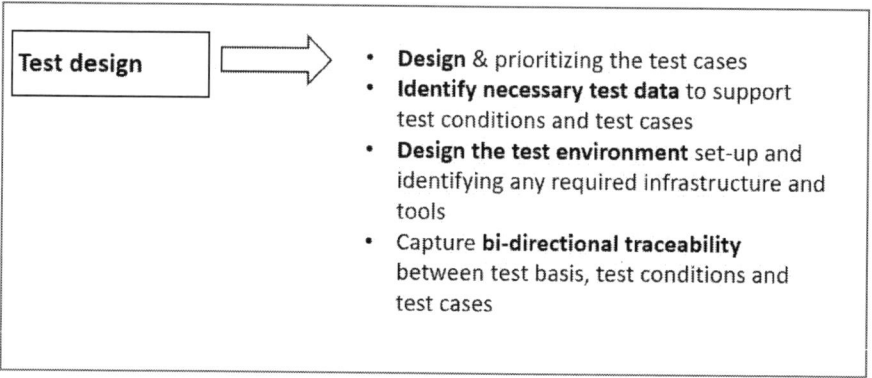

As with test analysis, test design can also have a potential benefit of the identification of similar types of defects in the test basis.

Test implementation

Test implementation is the activity where test cases are transformed into test procedures.

It has the following major tasks:

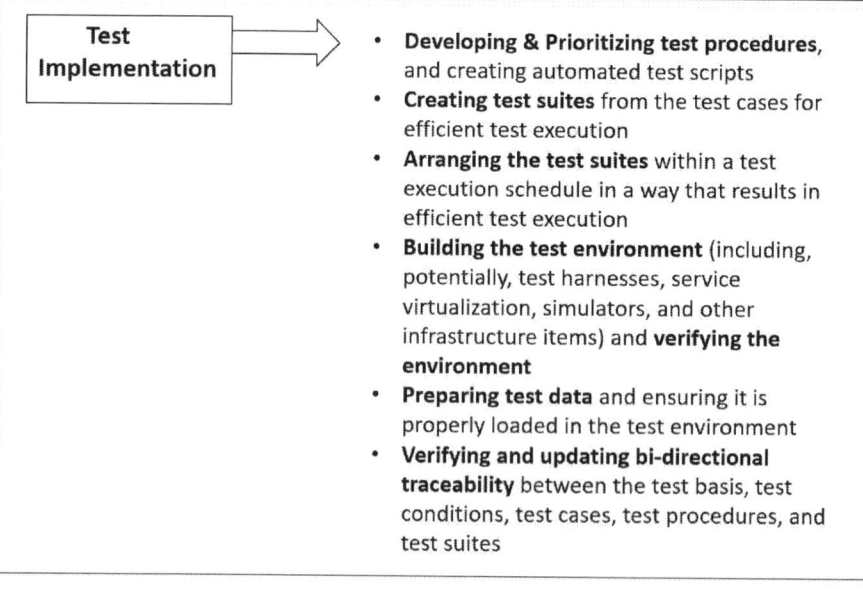

Test design and test implementation tasks are often combined.

In exploratory testing and other types of experience-based testing, test design and implementation may occur, and may be documented, as part of test execution. Exploratory testing may be based on test charters (produced as part of test analysis), and exploratory tests are executed immediately as they are designed and implemented.

Test execution

Test execution is the activity where test cases are run.

It has the following major tasks:

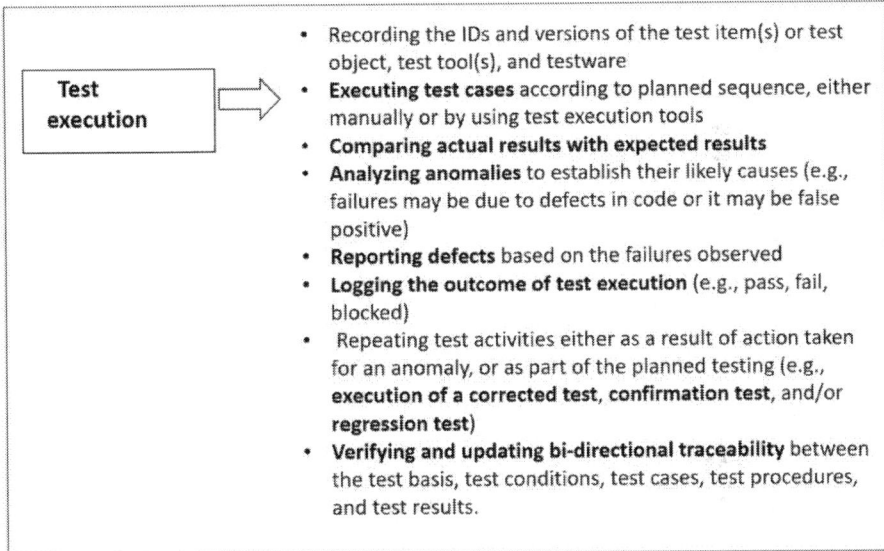

- Recording the IDs and versions of the test item(s) or test object, test tool(s), and testware
- **Executing test cases** according to planned sequence, either manually or by using test execution tools
- **Comparing actual results with expected results**
- **Analyzing anomalies** to establish their likely causes (e.g., failures may be due to defects in code or it may be false positive)
- **Reporting defects** based on the failures observed
- **Logging the outcome of test execution** (e.g., pass, fail, blocked)
- Repeating test activities either as a result of action taken for an anomaly, or as part of the planned testing (e.g., **execution of a corrected test, confirmation test,** and/or **regression test**)
- **Verifying and updating bi-directional traceability** between the test basis, test conditions, test cases, test procedures, and test results.

Test completion

Test completion activities occur at project milestones such as when a software system is released, a test project is completed (or cancelled), an Agile project iteration is finished, a test level is completed, or a maintenance release has been completed.

Test completion has the following major tasks:

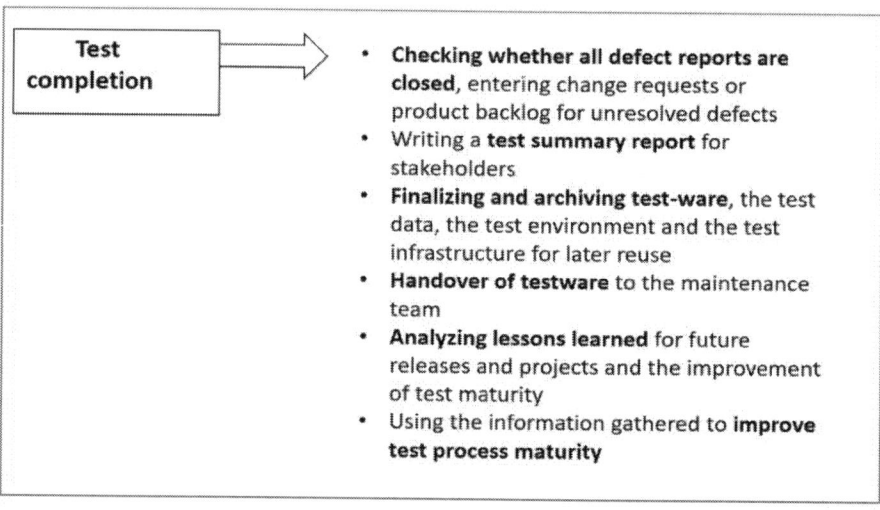

1.4.3 Test Work Products

Test work products are created as part of the test process. ISO standard (ISO/IEC/IEEE 29119-3) may also serve as a guideline for test work products. Most of the test work products described can be captured and managed using test management tools and defect management tools.

Test planning work products

Test planning work products include:

- Master test plan.
- Test plan for each test level

The test plan includes information about the test basis, to which the other test work products will be related via traceability information.

Test monitoring and control work products

Test monitoring and control work products typically include

- Test progress reports (produced on an ongoing and/or a regular basis)
- Test summary reports (produced at various completion milestones).

Test monitoring and control work products should also address project management concerns, such as task completion, resource allocation and usage, and effort.

Test analysis work products

Test analysis work products include:

- Defined and prioritized test conditions
- Creation of test charters (for exploratory testing)

Test analysis may also result in the discovery and reporting of defects in the test basis.

Test design work products

Test design work products include:

- Test cases
- Identification of the necessary test data
- Design of the test environment
- Identification of infrastructure and tools

Test implementation work products

Test implementation work products include:

- Test procedures and the sequencing of those test procedures
- Test suites
- A test execution schedule

Test execution work products

Test execution work products include:

- Documentation of the status of individual test cases or test procedures (e.g., ready to run, pass, fail, blocked, etc.)

- Defect reports
- Documentation about which test item(s), test object(s), test tools, and testware were involved in the testing

Test completion work products

Test completion work products include:

- Test summary reports
- Action items for improvement of subsequent projects or iterations
- Change requests or product backlog items
- Finalized testware

1.4.4 Traceability between the Test Basis and Test Work Products

It is important to establish and maintain traceability throughout the test process between each element of the test basis and the various test work products associated with that element. In addition to the evaluation of test coverage, good traceability supports:

- Analyzing the impact of changes
- Making testing auditable
- Meeting IT governance criteria
- Improving the understandability of test progress reports and test summary reports to include the status of elements of the test basis (e.g., requirements that passed their tests, requirements that failed their tests, and requirements that have pending tests)
- Relating the technical aspects of testing to stakeholders in terms that they can understand
- Providing information to assess product quality, process capability, and project progress against business goals

1.5 The psychology of testing

Similar to other software development activities software testing also involves human beings. Therefore, human psychology has important effects on software testing.

1.5.1 Human Psychology and Testing

Although testing contributes greatly to project progress and product quality it is sometimes perceived as a destructive activity due to following psychological factors:

- **Confirmation bias** - It is difficult for humans to become aware of errors committed by themselves. For example, since developers expect their code to be correct, they have a confirmation bias that makes it difficult to accept that the code is incorrect.
- **Cognitive bias** - This may make it difficult for people to understand or accept information produced by testing.
- It is a common human trait to blame the bearer of bad news, and information produced by testing often contains bad news.
- Some people may perceive testing results as a criticism of the product and of its author. For example, when testers identify defects during testing, these defects may be seen as a criticism of the product and author rather than the status of product quality.

To try to reduce these perceptions, information about defects and failures should be communicated in a constructive way. This may reduce the tension between the testers and the other project team members such as, analysts, product owners, designers, and developers. This is applicable for both static and dynamic testing.

Testers and test managers need to have good interpersonal skills to be able to communicate effectively about defects, failures, test results, test progress, and risks, and to build positive relationships with colleagues. Ways to communicate well include the following examples:

- Start with collaboration rather than battles. Remind everyone of the common goal of better-quality systems.
- Emphasize the benefits of testing. For example, for the authors, defect information can help them improve their work products and their skills. For the organization, defects found and fixed during testing will save time and money and reduce overall risk to product quality.

- Communicate test results and other findings in a neutral, fact-focused way without criticizing the person who created the defective item. Write objective and factual defect reports and review findings.
- Try to understand how the other person feels and the reasons they may react negatively to the information.
- Confirm that the other person has understood what has been said and vice versa.

It is important to clearly state the objectives of testing at the outset of a project. These objectives may include finding as many defects as possible. Clearly defining the right set of test objectives has important psychological implications. Most people tend to align their plans and behaviors with the objectives set by the team, management, and other stakeholders. It is also important that testers adhere to these objectives with minimal personal bias.

1.5.2 Tester's and Developer's Mindsets

The primary objective of development is to design and build a product whereas, the objectives of testing include verifying and validating the product and finding defects prior to release.

These are different sets of objectives which require different mindsets. Bringing these mindsets together helps to achieve a higher level of product quality.

A mindset reflects an individual's assumptions and preferred methods for decision making and problem-solving.

- **A tester's mindset** should include curiosity, professional pessimism, a critical eye, attention to detail, and a motivation for good and positive communications and relationships. A tester's mindset tends to grow and mature as the tester gains experience.
- **A developer's mindset** may include some of the elements of a tester's mindset, but successful developers are often more interested in designing and building solutions than in contemplating what might be wrong with those solutions. In addition, confirmation bias makes it difficult to find mistakes in their own work. With the right mindset, developers are able to test their own code.

Different software development lifecycle models often have different ways of organizing the testers and test activities. However, having some of the test activities done by independent testers increases defect detection effectiveness, which is particularly important for large, complex, or safety-critical systems.

Independent testers bring a perspective that is different than that of the work product authors (i.e., business analysts, product owners, designers, and programmers) since they have different cognitive biases from the authors.

Chapter 5 provides more information on Independent testing.

Key exam take-out
Developers and testers have different mindsets as development and testing have different objectives.

1.6 Relevant glossary terms and keywords

Glossary term	Definition
Coverage	The degree to which specified coverage items have been determined or have been exercised by a test suite expressed as a percentage.
Defect	An imperfection or deficiency in a work product where it does not meet its requirements or specifications. [IEEE 1044]
Debugging	The process of finding, analyzing and removing the causes of failures in software.
Error, Mistake	A human action that produces an incorrect result. [ISO 24765]
Exit criteria	The set of conditions for officially completing a defined task.
Exhaustive testing	A test approach in which the test suite comprises all combinations of input values and preconditions.
Failure	An event in which a component or system does not perform a required function within specified limits. [ISO 24765]
Functional testing	Testing performed to evaluate if a component or system satisfies functional requirements. [ISO 24765]
Non-functional testing	Testing performed to evaluate that a component or system complies with non-functional requirements.
Regression testing	A type of change-related testing to detect whether defects have been introduced or uncovered in unchanged areas of the software.
Requirement	A provision that contains criteria to be fulfilled. [ISO 24765]
Risk	A factor that could result in future negative consequences; usually expressed as impact and likelihood.
Risk-based testing	Testing in which the management, selection, prioritization, and use of testing activities and resources are based on corresponding risk types and risk levels. [ISO 29119]
Root cause	A source of a defect such that if it is removed, the occurrence of the defect type is decreased or removed. [CMMI]

Glossary term	Definition
Quality	The degree to which a component or system satisfies the stated and implied needs of its various stakeholders.
Quality Assurance	Activities focused on providing confidence that quality requirements will be fulfilled. [ISO 24765]
Quality Control	A set of activities designed to evaluate the quality of a component or system.
Quality Management	Coordinated activities to direct and control an organization with regard to quality that include establishing a quality policy and quality objectives, quality planning, quality control, quality assurance, and quality improvement.
Test basis	The body of knowledge used as the basis for test analysis and design.
Test case	A set of preconditions, inputs, actions (where applicable), expected results and postconditions, developed based on test conditions. [ISO 29119]
Test data	Data needed for test execution.
Test execution	The activity that runs a test on a component or system producing actual results.
Test log	A chronological record of relevant details about the execution of tests. [ISO 24765]
Test object	The component or system to be tested.
Test objective	The reason or purpose of testing.
Test oracle	A source to determine expected results to compare with the actual result of the system under test.
Test Procedure	A sequence of test cases in execution order, and any associated actions that may be required to set up the initial preconditions and any wrap up activities post execution. [ISO 29119]
Test process	The set of interrelated activities comprising of test planning, test monitoring and control, test analysis, test design, test implementation, test execution, and test completion.
Test suite	A set of test scripts or test procedures to be executed in a specific test run.
Testware	Work products produced during the test process for use in planning, designing, executing, evaluating and reporting on testing.

Glossary term	Definition
Testing	The process consisting of all lifecycle activities, both static and dynamic, concerned with planning, preparation, and evaluation of a component or system and related work products to determine that they satisfy specified requirements, to demonstrate that they are fit for purpose and to detect defects.
Traceability	The degree to which a relationship can be established between two or more work products.
Validation	Confirmation by examination and through provision of objective evidence that the requirements for a specific intended use or application have been fulfilled. [ISO 9000]
Verification	Confirmation by examination and through provision of objective evidence that specified requirements have been fulfilled. [ISO 9000]

1.7 Quiz

Question 1

Which of the following would **NOT** be considered as a valid objective for testing?

a) To comply with standards.
b) To confirm the system works as expected.
c) To find all the defects in the system under test.
d) To provide sufficient information to the stakeholders.

Question 2

Which of the following TWO are part for ISTQB Test analysis activity?

a) Identify defects in test basis.
b) Identify the infrastructure and tool required for testing
c) Identify the test data to support test cases.
d) Creating bi-directional traceability between the test basis and the test conditions.

Question 3

Differentiate the following testing terms (1-4) by mapping them to the right examples (A-D).

1. Error
2. Defect
3. Failure
4. Effect

A. The bank is penalized by the banking regulatory board.
B. The customer is charged more interest on their home loan accounts.
C. The program is using the wrong algorithm for home loan interest calculation.
D. The business analyst entered the wrong formula for home loan calculation in the requirement.

a) 1A, 2C, 3B, 4D.
b) 1D, 2B, 3A, 4C.
c) 1D, 2C, 3B, 4A.
d) 1A, 2C, 3D, 4B.

Question 4

Which of the following statements BEST describes one of the seven key principles of software testing?

a) Customer will be satisfied with the system if the majority of defects are found and fixed before release.
b) If the testing is stared earlier in the project it will increase the overall cost of the project.
c) Automated regression test can find defects over a period of time.
d) Testing cannot prove the absence of the defects in the system.

Question 5

Which of the following are examples of Test implementation work products?

I. Test cases.
II. Design of test environment.
III. Test suites.
IV. Test execution schedule.

a) I & IV.
b) I & III.
c) II & III
d) III & IV.

Question 6

Which of the following statement is TRUE about quality assurance?

a) Quality assurance involves various activities including test activities.
b) Quality assurance includes all activities that direct and control an organization with regard to quality.
c) Quality assurance does not ensure that the organization's standards are followed.
d) Quality assurance focuses on root cause analysis and removal of defects.

Question 7

Which one of the following is the BEST description for test monitoring?

a) The activity that checks the status of testing activities, identifies any variances from planned or expected, and reports status to stakeholders.
b) The activity that derives and specifies test cases from test conditions.
c) The activity that identifies test conditions by analyzing the test basis.
d) The activity that prepares the testware needed for test execution based on test analysis and design.

1.8 Answers

1	2	3	4	5	6	7
C	A, D	C	D	D	D	A

Question 1

FL-1.1.1 (K1) Identify typical objectives of testing

Justification

a) Not correct – This is a valid objective for testing. (Syllabus 1.1.1)
b) Not correct – This is a valid objective for testing. (Syllabus 1.1.1)
c) **Correct** – This is not a valid objective for testing. Principle #1 states that exhaustive testing is not possible therefore finding **all the defects** in the system is not possible.
d) Not correct – This is a valid objective for testing (Syllabus 1.1.1)

Question 2

FL-1.4.2 (K2) Describe the test activities and respective tasks within the test process

Justification

a) **Correct** – Evaluating the test basis to identify various defects is part of Test analysis. Syllabus 1.4.2
b) Not correct – this activity is part of Test design.
c) Not correct – this activity is part of Test design.
d) **Correct** – This activity is performed during the Test analysis. Syllabus 1.4.2.

Question 3

FL-1.2.3 (K2) Distinguish between error, defect, and failure

Justification

An error is a mistake by a person which can lead to the introduction of the defect. In this case, the business analyst has made the mistake which resulted in the wrong requirement. **(1D)**

The defect is an imperfection or deficiency in a work product or code where it does not meet the requirements or specifications. In this case, the program using the wrong algorithm for home loan interest calculation is a defect. **(2C)**

Failure is an event in which a component or system does not perform a required function within specified limits. In this case, it is the incorrect interest calculated for the customers home loan account. **(3B)**

The Effect is the consequence of failures. In this case, bank penalized by the banking regulatory board is the consequences of the customer charged more on the home loan interest. (failure). **(4A)**

Thus:

a) Not correct
b) Not correct
c) **Correct**
d) Not correct

Question 4

FL-1.3.1 (K2) Explain the seven testing principles

Justification

- This is contradicting Principle#7. Finding and fixing a large number of defects can't ensure the success of a system as it may not be able to fulfill the users' needs and expectations. (Syllabus 1.3)
- This is contradicting Principle#3. Testing early in the software development lifecycle helps reduce or eliminate costly changes. (Syllabus 1.3)
- This is contradicting Principle#5. Same tests (automated or manual) repeated over and over again can't find defects. (Syllabus 1.3)
- This is true. Principle#1 -Testing can show that defects are present, but cannot prove that there are no more defects. (Syllabus 1.3)

Thus:

a) Not correct
b) Not correct
c) Not correct
d) **Correct**

Question 5

FL-1.4.3 (K2) Differentiate the work products that support the test process

Justification

I. **Test cases** are Test design work product. Syllabus 1.4.3.
II. **Design of test environment** is Test design work product. Syllabus 1.4.3.
III. **Test suites** are Test implementation work product. Syllabus 1.4.3.
IV. **Test execution schedule** is a Test implementation work product. Syllabus 1.4.3.

Thus:

a) Not correct
b) Not correct
c) Not correct
d) **Correct**

Question 6

FL-1.2.2 (K2) Describe the relationship between testing and quality assurance and give examples of how testing contributes to higher quality

Justification

a) This is **false**. It is not quality assurance but quality control which including test activities, that support the achievement of appropriate levels of quality. Syllabus 1.2.2
b) This is **false**. It is not quality assurance but quality management which all activities that direct and control an organization with regard to quality. Syllabus 1.2.2
c) This is **false**. Quality assurance is typically focused on adherence to proper organizations processes. Syllabus 1.2.2
d) This is **true**. Quality assurance focuses on root cause analysis to detect and remove the causes of defects. Syllabus 1.2.2

Question 7

FL-1.x (K1) Keywords Chapter 1

Justification

a) **Correct** – This is the definition of test monitoring according to Glossary.
b) Not correct – This is the definition of test design according to Glossary.
c) Not correct – This is the definition of test analysis according to Glossary
d) Not correct – This is the definition of test implementation from Glossary.

2 Testing Throughout the Software Development Lifecycle

Learning Objectives for Testing Throughout the Software Development Lifecycle 46
2.1 Software development Lifecycle models..47
    2.1.1 Software Development and Software Testing........................47
    2.1.2 Software Development Lifecycle Models in Context.................52
2.2 Test levels 53
    2.2.1 Component / unit testing...54
    2.2.2 Integration testing 56
    2.2.3 System testing...61
    2.2.4 Acceptance testing 63
2.3 Test types 68
    2.3.1 Functional Testing...68
    2.3.2 Non-functional testing 69
    2.3.3 White box testing 70
    2.3.4 Change-related testing 71
    2.3.5 Test Types and Test Levels 72
2.4 Maintenance testing 74
    2.4.1 Triggers for Maintenance..74
    2.4.2 Impact Analysis for Maintenance 76
2.5 Relevant glossary terms and keywords...77
2.6 Quiz 81
2.7 Answers 83

Learning Objectives for Testing Throughout the Software Development Lifecycle

This Chapter considers testing as part of overall software development.

Following learning objectives are covered in this chapter:

2.1 Software Development Lifecycle Models

FL-2.1.1 (K2) Explain the relationships between software development activities and test activities in the software development lifecycle

FL-2.1.2 (K1) Identify reasons why software development lifecycle models must be adapted to the context of project and product characteristics

2.2 Test Levels

FL-2.2.1 (K2) Compare the different test levels from the perspective of objectives, test basis, test objects, typical defects and failures, and approaches and responsibilities

2.3 Test Types

FL-2.3.1 (K2) Compare functional, non-functional, and white-box testing

FL-2.3.2 (K1) Recognize that functional, non-functional, and white-box tests occur at any test level

FL-2.3.3 (K2) Compare the purposes of confirmation testing and regression testing

2.4 Maintenance Testing

FL-2.4.1 (K2) Summarize triggers for maintenance testing

FL-2.4.2 (K2) Describe the role of impact analysis in maintenance testing

2.1 Software Development Lifecycle Models

A software development lifecycle model describes the types of activity performed at each stage in a software development project, and how these activities relate to one another logically and chronologically. There are a number of different software development lifecycle models, each of which requires different approaches to testing.

2.1.1 Software Development and Software Testing

It is important for the tester to be familiar with the common software development lifecycle models so that appropriate test activities can take place.

In any software development life cycle model, there are several characteristics of good testing:

- For every development activity, there is a corresponding testing activity
- Each test level has test objectives specific to that level
- The analysis and design of tests for a given test level should begin during the corresponding development activity
- Testers participate in discussions to define and refine requirements and design and are involved in reviewing work products (e.g., requirements, design, user stories, etc.) as soon as drafts are available.

Irrespective of the software development lifecycle model, test activities should start in the early stages of the lifecycle, adhering to the testing principle of early testing.

This syllabus categorizes common software development lifecycle models as follows:

- Sequential development models
- Iterative and incremental development models

Sequential development model

A sequential development model describes the software development process as a linear, sequential flow of activities. This means that any phase in the development process should only begin when the previous phase is complete. In theory, there is no overlap of phases, but in most of the projects there is a slight overlap of phases. This enables some early feedback from the following phase.

Examples of sequential development model are:

- Waterfall model
- V-model

Waterfall model

In the Waterfall model, there is a separate phase for each development activities. The typical phases in waterfall model are requirements analysis, design, coding and testing.

These phases are completed one after the other. In this model, test activities only occur after all the development activities have been completed.

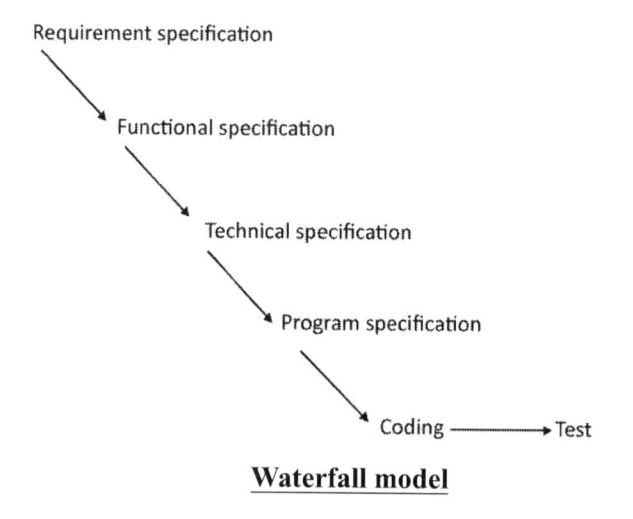

```
Requirement specification
        ↘
            Functional specification
                    ↘
                        Technical specification
                                ↘
                                    Program specification
                                            ↘
                                                Coding ——→ Test
```

Waterfall model

V- model

The V-model integrates the test process throughout the development process to implement the principle of early testing.

The V-model includes test levels associated with each corresponding development phase; A common type of V-model is shown below:

V-model

```
Test basis                Requirements         User Acceptance Test Level                    Acceptance
for UAT          →        elicitation               (User confidence)                        testing
Testing

Test basis    Functional
for System    Requirements               System Test Level                                   System
Testing       elicitation      (Functional and non-functional behaviour)                     testing

Test basis          Technical            Integration Test Level
for Integration →   Requirements         (Interfaces between                                 Integration
Testing             elicitation              components)                                     testing

Test basis          Preparation          Unit Test Level
for Unit       →    of program           (Individual                                         Unit
Testing             specification          Units)                                            testing

                                           Coding
```

V-model

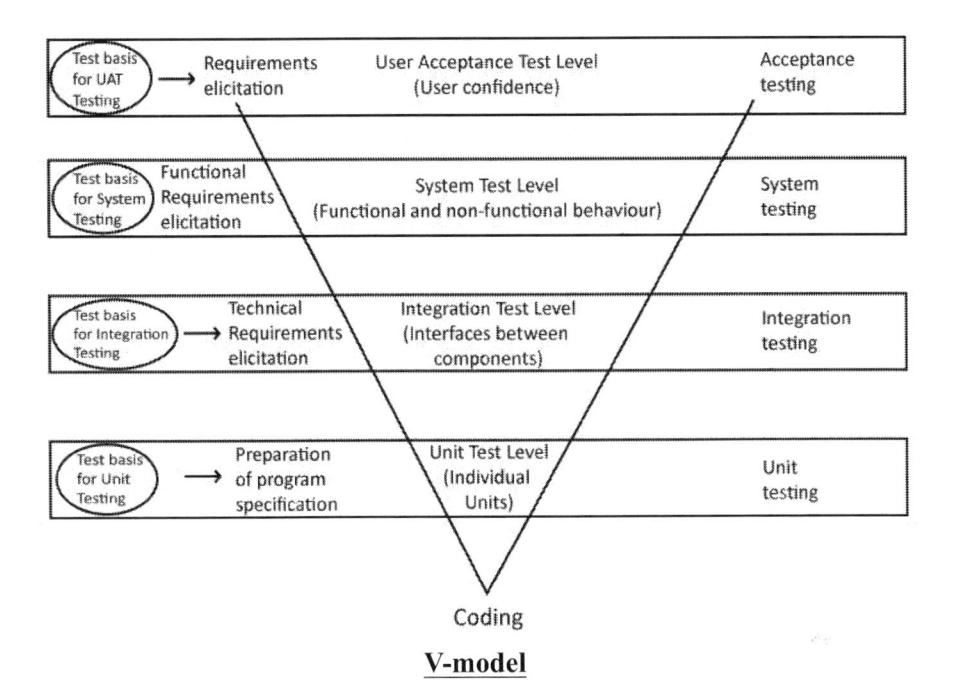

The activities on the left-hand side of the V-model focuses on work-product creation for elaborating the initial requirements and then providing more technical detail for the development:

- Requirement specification—capturing of user needs.
- Functional specification—definition of functions required to meet user needs.
- Technical specification—technical design or architecture of functions identified in the functional specification.
- Program specification—detailed design of each module or unit to be built to meet the required functionality.

There is a relationship between the work products on the left-hand side, and the testing activities on the right-hand side. Each work product can be **verified** by using static testing techniques (e.g. reviews) ensuring that the requirements as stated have been met. **Verification** helps to ensure that the product is built in the right way.

The middle of the V-model shows that planning for testing can start as soon as the work-products for a particular development phase are ready. For example, once the requirement specifications are ready, planning for acceptance testing can be started.

The right-hand side focuses on the testing activities (**dynamic testing**).

- o   Testing against the program specification takes place at the unit testing stage.
- o   Testing against the technical specification takes place at the integration testing stage
- o   Testing against the functional specification takes place at the system testing stage.
- o   Testing against the requirement specification takes place at the acceptance testing stage.

Right-hand side of the V- model **validates** the requirement using the dynamic testing techniques. **Validation** ensures that requirements, as stated, have been met.

> **Key exam take-out**
>
> **Verification** checks that the product is being **built in the right way.**
>
> **Validation** checks that the **right product is being built**.

Iterative and incremental development models

Iterative development is the process of establishing requirements, designing, building and testing a system, done as a series of smaller incremental developments. In iterative development, the requirements can be clarified or discovered as the number of iterations increases. The approach is to 'build a little, test a little'. Each iteration provides feedback for the next iteration. Once a particular iteration has been completed the testing of the new elements of software must be tested with the existing unchanged software, thus it is necessary to perform regression testing after every single iteration.

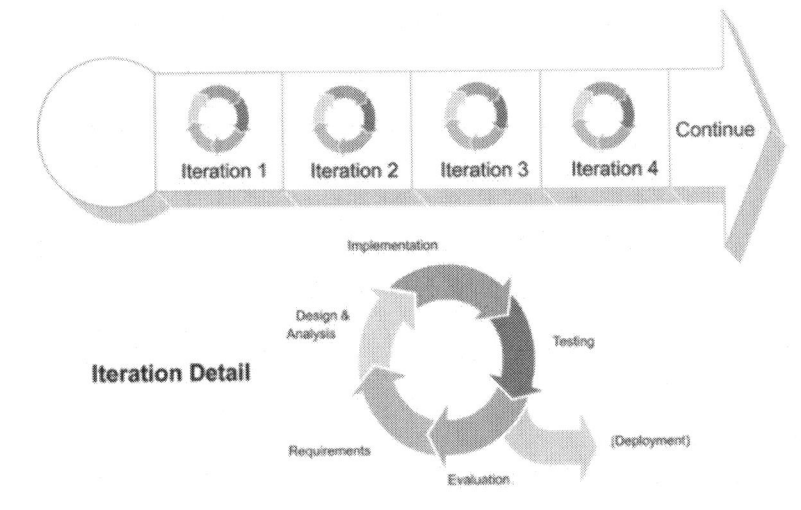

Iterative & Incremental development

Examples are:

- **Rational Unified Process**: Each iteration tends to be relatively long (e.g., two to three months), and the feature increments are correspondingly large, such as two or three groups of related features
- **Scrum**: Each iteration tends to be relatively short (e.g., hours, days, or a few weeks), and the feature increments are correspondingly small, such as a few enhancements and/or two or three new features
- **Kanban**: Implemented with or without fixed-length iterations, which can deliver either a single enhancement or feature upon completion, or can group features together to release at once
- **Spiral:** Involves creating experimental increments. Some of these increments may be re-worked or even discarded in subsequent development work

The increment produced by an iteration may be tested at several levels as part of its development. An increment added to previously developed & tested functionality, forms a growing partial system, which should also be tested.

Regression testing is increasingly important on all iterations after the first one. Verification and validation can be carried out on each increment.

Incremental development involves establishing requirements, designing, building, and testing a system in pieces, which means that the software's features grow incrementally. The size of these feature increments varies, with some methods having larger pieces and some smaller pieces. The feature increments can be as small as a single change to a user interface screen or new query option.

2.1.2 Software Development Lifecycle Models in Context

Software development lifecycle models must be selected and adapted to the context of project and product characteristics. An appropriate software development lifecycle model is selected and adapted based on the following:

- Project goal
- Type of product being developed
- Business priorities (e.g., time-to-market)
- Identified product and project risks

Test levels can be combined or reorganized depending on the nature of the project or the system architecture.

Example: For the integration of a commercial off-the-shelf (COTS) software product into a system following testing may be done by the buyer:

- Integration testing at the system level (e.g. integration to the infrastructure and other systems),
- Acceptance testing (functional and/or non-functional, and user and/or operational testing).

In addition, software development lifecycle models themselves may be combined. For example, a **V- model** may be used for the development and testing of the **backend systems** and their integrations, while an **Agile development model** may be used to develop and test **the front-end user interface (UI) and functionality**. Prototyping may be used early in a project, with an incremental development model adopted once the experimental phase is complete.

Internet of Things (IoT) systems, which consist of many different objects, such as devices, products, and services, typically apply separate software development lifecycle models for each object. Additionally, the software development lifecycle of such objects places a stronger emphasis on the later phases of the software development lifecycle after they have been introduced to operational use (e.g., operate, update, and decommission phases).

Software development models must be adapted to the context of project and product characteristics due to following reasons:

- There may be differences in product risks of systems (complex or simple project)
- There can be many business units which are part of a project or program (combination of sequential and Agile development)
- There may be a short time to deliver a product to the market (merging test levels and/or integration of test types in test levels)

2.2 Test levels

Test levels are groups of test activities that are organized and managed together. Each test level is an instance of the test process, consisting of the activities performed in relation to the software at a given level of development. Test levels are related to other activities within the software development lifecycle. The test levels covered in this syllabus are:

- Component testing
- Integration testing
- System testing
- Acceptance testing

Test levels are characterized by the following attributes:

- Specific objectives
- Test basis, referenced to derive test cases
- Test object (i.e., what is being tested)
- Typical defects and failures
- Specific approaches and responsibilities

For every test level, a suitable test environment is required. For example, in acceptance testing, a production-like test environment is ideal, whereas for the component testing the developers typically use the same environment where they have developed the components (development environment).

To get a better understanding of test levels we will use a sample application called E-SYSTEM. This application allows customers to check their electricity usage online.

There are three components/units in this application

Login - This is used to enable sign-in for the customers using their LoginID/password

Usage – This is to display the customer's current meter reading

Logout - This is used to sign-out the customer from the application.

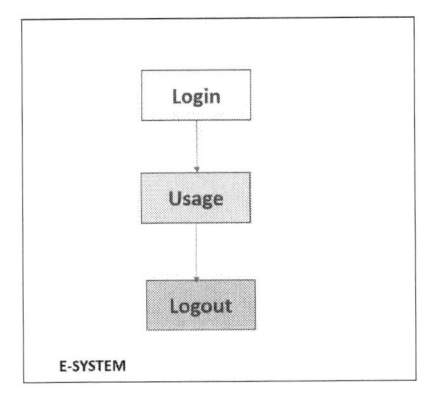

2.2.1 Component / unit testing

Objectives of component testing

Component testing (also known as unit or module testing) focuses on components that are separately testable. Objectives of component testing include:

- Reducing risk
- Verifying whether the functional and non-functional behaviors of the component are as designed and specified
- Building confidence in the component's quality
- Finding defects in the component
- Preventing defects from escaping to higher test levels

In incremental and iterative development models (e.g., Agile) where code changes are ongoing, automated component regression tests play a key role in building confidence that changes have not broken the existing components.

Component testing is often done in isolation from the rest of the component of the system, Component testing may cover functionality (e.g., correctness of calculations), non-functional characteristics (e.g., searching for memory leaks), and structural properties (e.g., decision testing).

If we refer our sample application E-SYSTEM, developers will develop Login, Usage and Logout components in isolation with other components. The testing for each module will also be done independent of each other.

| Login | Usage | Logout |

Test objects

Typical test objects for component testing include:

- Components, units or modules
- Code and data structures
- Classes
- Database modules

Test basis

Typically, the work products used as the basis for component testing would be:

- Detailed design
- Code
- Data model
- Component specification

Specific approaches and responsibilities

Component testing is usually performed by the developer after the code is written for a component. However, in some Agile and sequential development test-first approach is also used, where automated component test cases are created prior to coding.

Test-driven development (TDD) is an example of test-first approach which starts with creating automated test cases for component tests. After that small pieces of code are built and integrated. The component tests are then executed, correcting any issues, and re-factoring the code. This process continues until the component has been completely built and all component tests are passing.

Typical defects and failures

Examples of typical defects and failures for component testing include:

- Incorrect functionality
- Data flow problems
- Incorrect code and logic

Defects found at component testing are typically fixed as soon as they are found, without formally recording defects.

Key exam take-out

- The purpose of **component testing** is to ensure that the code written for the component meets its specification, prior to its integration with other components.
- Performed by developers who have coded the component.
- Conducted in the development environment.
- Defects found and fixed as soon as they are found without going through a defect management process.

2.2.2 Integration testing

Objectives of integration testing

Integration testing **focuses on the interaction between components or systems**. Objectives of integration testing include:

- Reducing risk
- Verifying whether the functional and non-functional behaviors of the interfaces are as designed and specified
- Building confidence in the quality of the interfaces
- Finding defects (which may be in the interfaces themselves or within the components or systems)
- Preventing defects from escaping to higher test levels

As with component testing, in some cases, automated integration regression tests provide confidence that changes have not broken existing interfaces, components, or systems.

There are two different levels of integration testing:

- **Component integration testing** focuses on the interactions between software components and is done after component testing.
- **System integration testing** focuses on the interactions between different systems, packages and microservices and mostly done after system testing or in parallel with ongoing system test activities. System integration testing can also cover interactions with the interfaces provided by external organizations (e.g., web services). In this case, the developing organization does not control the external interfaces, which can create various challenges for testing (e.g. arranging for test environments, etc.)

Test basis

Typically, the software development work products used as the basis for integration testing would be:

- Software and system design
- Architecture at component or system level
- Sequence diagrams
- Interface and communication protocol specifications
- Use cases
- Workflows
- External interface definitions

Test objects

Typical test objects for the integration test level would be:

- Sub-systems
- Database implementation
- Infrastructure
- Interfaces
- APIs
- Microservices

Specific approaches and responsibilities

Component integration testing is often the responsibility of developers whereas, system integration testing is generally the responsibility of testers. Testers performing system integration testing should understand the system architecture and should have influenced integration planning.

Component integration tests and system integration tests should concentrate on the integration itself. For example, if integrating module A with module B, tests should focus on the communication between the modules, not the functionality of the individual modules, as that should have been covered during component testing. If integrating system X with system Y, tests should focus on the communication between the systems, not the functionality of the individual systems, as that should have been covered during system testing. Functional, non-functional, and structural test types are applicable for integration testing.

There are three commonly used integration strategies, as follows:

Big-Bang Integration

This is where all the components are integrated in one step resulting in a complete system.

If Big-Bang integration is used for our sample application all the modules **Login, Usage and Logout** should be ready and then linked at once.

Top-Down Integration

This is where the system is built in stages, starting with components that call other components. Components that call others are usually placed above those that are called. Top-down integration testing will permit the tester to evaluate component interfaces, starting with those at the 'top'.

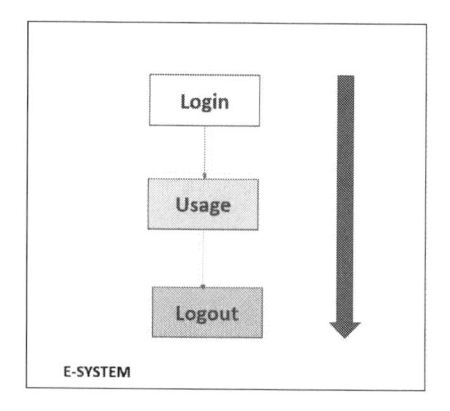

[Diagram: E-SYSTEM containing Login → Usage → Logout with downward arrow]

Top-down Integration

The control structure of a program can be represented in a diagram above. **Login** will call component **Usage**. The component **Usage** will be calling **logout** component. The integration order will be:

- Login, Usage
- Usage, Logout

In this case, while testing the first scenario, if the Usage component is not ready, a skeletal implementation of the component called stub will be created. **A stub is a passive component, called by other components**. In this case, this stub will just return two values "successful login" for right LoginID/password combination and "unsuccessful login" for wrong LoginID/password combination. These two values are sufficient to test the Login module.

Bottom-up Integration

This is the opposite of top-down integration and the components are integrated in bottom-up order.

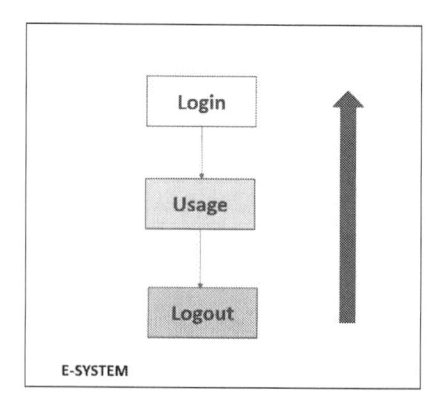

[Diagram: E-SYSTEM containing Login → Usage → Logout with upward arrow]

Bottom-up integration

The integration order will be:

- Logout, Usage,
- Usage, Login

In bottom-up integration when testing the first scenario if the **Usage** component is not built yet so we have to use a component called **driver** to replace it. **Drivers are Active component which are calling other components.** They are generally more complex than stubs. For system integration testing there is also a possibility that one of the external systems is not ready or not accessible for testing. In this case **simulators** are used to mimic these external systems.

In order to simplify defect isolation and detect defects early, integration should normally be incremental rather than "big bang". A risk analysis of the most complex interfaces can help to focus the integration testing.

The greater the scope of integration, the more difficult it becomes to isolate defects to a specific component or system, which may lead to increased risk and additional time for troubleshooting. This is one reason that continuous integration, where software is integrated on a component-by-component basis (i.e., functional integration), has become common practice. Such continuous integration often includes automated regression testing, ideally at multiple test levels.

Key exam take-out

A Stub is a skeletal or special-purpose implementation of a software component, used to develop or test a component that calls or is otherwise dependent on it. It replaces a "called" component.

A Driver is a software component or test tool that replaces a component that takes care of the control and/or the calling of a component or system.

A Simulator is a device, computer program or system used during testing, which behaves or operates like a given system when provided with a set of controlled inputs.

Typical defects and failures

Examples of typical defects and failures for component integration testing include:

- Incorrect data, missing data, or incorrect data encoding
- Incorrect sequencing or timing of interface calls

- Interface mismatch
- Failures in communication between components
- Unhandled or improperly handled communication failures between components
- Incorrect assumptions about the meaning, units, or boundaries of the data being passed between components

---

Key exam take-out
• The purpose of **component integration testing** is to expose defects in the interactions between integrated components and is done after component testing. • Performed by the developers who have coded the components • Conducted in the development environment

If our sample application E-SYSTEM is passing the USAGE data to an external application BILLING which processes this information to generate an invoice for the customer. The scope of system integration testing will be to verify that the data is passed correctly to the BILLING system. If the BILLING system is not ready or not accessible for testing, then we may need to use a **simulator** to mimic this system.

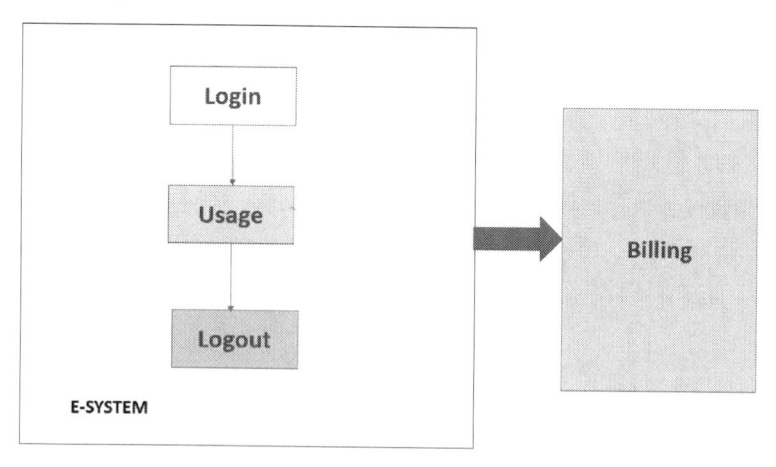

```
E-SYSTEM
  Login
    ↓
  Usage  ──────→  Billing
    ↓
  Logout
```

Examples of typical defects and failures for system integration testing include:

- Inconsistent message structures between systems
- Incorrect data, missing data, or incorrect data encoding
- Interface mismatch
- Failures in communication between systems
- Unhandled or improperly handled communication failures between systems

> **Key exam take-out**
> - The purpose of **system integration testing** is to test interactions between different systems or between hardware and software.
> - Performed by a tester who understand the overall architecture
> - Conducted in a testing environment.

2.2.3 System testing

Objectives of system testing

System testing focuses on the **behavior and capabilities of a whole system** or product, often considering the end-to-end tasks the system can perform and the non-functional behaviors it exhibits while performing those tasks. Objectives of system testing include:

- Reducing risk
- Verifying whether the functional and non-functional behaviors of the system are as designed and specified
- Validating that the system is complete and will work as expected
- Building confidence in the quality of the system as a whole
- Finding defects
- Preventing defects from escaping to higher test levels or production
- Verifying data quality (for certain systems)

System testing often produces information that is used by stakeholders to make release decisions. System testing may also satisfy legal or regulatory requirements or standards.

The test environment should ideally correspond to the final target or production environment.

Test basis

Therefore, typical software development work products used as test basis for system testing might be:

- System and software requirement specifications (functional and non-functional)
- Risk analysis reports
- Use cases
- Epics and user stories
- Models of system behavior
- State diagrams
- System and user manuals

Test objects

Typical test objects for system testing include:

- Applications
- Hardware/software systems
- Operating systems
- System Under Test (SUT)
- System configuration and configuration data

Typical defects and failures

Examples of typical defects and failures for system testing include:

- Incorrect calculations
- Incorrect or unexpected system functional or non-functional behavior
- Incorrect control and/or data flows within the system
- Failure to properly and completely carry out end-to-end functional tasks
- Failure of the system to work properly in the system environment(s)
- Failure of the system to work as described in system and user manuals

Specific approaches and responsibilities

System testing should focus on the overall, end-to-end behavior of the system as a whole. System testing should investigate both the **functional and non-functional** requirements of the system.

System testing should use the most appropriate techniques (see chapter 4) for the aspect(s) of the system to be tested. For example, a decision table may be created to verify whether functional behavior is as described in business rules.

Independent testers typically carry out system testing relying heavily on specifications. Defects in specifications (e.g., missing user stories, incorrectly stated business requirements, etc.) can lead to a lack of understanding or disagreements about the expected system behavior. Such situations can cause false positives and false negatives, which waste time and reduce defect detection effectiveness, respectively. Early involvement of testers in reviews of specifications can help to reduce these incidences.

Key exam take-out

- The purpose of **system testing** is to validate the behavior of the system as a whole
- Performed by the Independent testers
- Conducted in a testing environment

2.2.4 Acceptance testing

Objectives of acceptance testing

Acceptance testing, like system testing, typically focuses on the behavior and capabilities of a whole system or product. Objectives of acceptance testing include:

- Establishing confidence in the quality of the system as a whole
- Validating that the system is complete and will work as expected
- Verifying that functional and non-functional behaviors of the system are as specified

Acceptance testing may produce information to assess the system's readiness for deployment and use by the customer (end-user). Defects may be found during acceptance testing, but finding defects is often not an objective, and finding a significant number of defects during acceptance testing may in some cases be considered a major project risk. Acceptance testing may also satisfy legal or regulatory requirements or standards.

Typical forms of acceptance testing include the following:

- User acceptance testing
- Operational acceptance testing
- Contractual and regulatory acceptance testing
- Alpha and beta testing.

Each of them is described below.

- **User acceptance testing (UAT)**

Acceptance testing of the system is typically focused on validating the fitness for use of the system by intended users in a real or simulated operational environment.

The main objective is building confidence that the users can use the system to meet their needs, fulfill requirements, and perform business processes with minimum difficulty, cost, and risk.

- **Operational acceptance testing (OAT)**

The acceptance of the system by the system administrators generally in a (simulated) production environment including:

- Testing of backup and restore
- Installing, uninstalling and upgrading
- Disaster recovery
- User management
- Maintenance tasks
- Data load and migration tasks
- Checks for security vulnerabilities
- Performance testing

The main objective of operational acceptance testing is building confidence that the operators or system administrators can keep the system working properly for the users in the operational environment, even under exceptional or difficult conditions.

- **Contractual and regulatory acceptance testing**

Contractual acceptance testing is performed against a contract's acceptance criteria for producing custom-developed software. Acceptance criteria should be defined when the parties agree to the contract. Contractual acceptance testing is often performed by users or by independent testers.

Regulatory acceptance testing is performed against any regulations that must be adhered to, such as government, legal, or safety regulations. Regulatory acceptance testing is often performed by users or by independent testers, sometimes with the results being witnessed or audited by regulatory agencies.

The main objective of contractual and regulatory acceptance testing is building confidence that contractual or regulatory compliance has been achieved.

- **Alpha and beta testing**

Alpha and beta testing are typically used by developers of commercial off-the-shelf (COTS) software who want to get feedback from potential or existing users, customers, and/or operators before the software product is put on the market.

Alpha testing is performed at the developing organization's site, not by the development team, but by potential or existing customers, and/or operators or an independent test team.

Beta testing is performed by potential or existing customers, and/or operators at their own locations. Beta testing may come after alpha testing, or may occur without any preceding alpha testing.

One objective of alpha and beta testing is building confidence among potential or existing customers of the system. Another objective is to detect defects related to the conditions and environment(s) if they can't be replicated by the development team.

Test basis

Typical test basis for acceptance testing are:
- Business processes
- User or business requirements
- Regulations, legal contracts and standards
- Use cases and/or user stories
- System requirements
- System or user documentation
- Installation procedures
- Risk analysis reports

In addition, as a test basis for deriving test cases for operational acceptance testing, one or more of the following work products can be used:

- Backup and restore procedures
- Disaster recovery procedures
- Non-functional requirements
- Operations documentation
- Deployment and installation instructions
- Performance targets
- Database packages
- Security standards or regulations

Typical test objects

Typical test objects for any form of acceptance testing include:

- System under test
- System configuration and configuration data
- Business processes for a fully integrated system
- Recovery systems and hot sites (for business continuity and disaster recovery testing)
- Operational and maintenance processes
- Forms
- Reports
- Existing and converted production data

Specific approaches and responsibilities

Acceptance testing is often the responsibility of the customers, business users, product owners, or operators of a system, and other stakeholders may be involved as well.

Acceptance testing is often thought of as the last test level in a sequential development lifecycle, but it may also occur at other times, for example:

- Acceptance testing of a Commercial Off The Shelf (COTS) software product may be done when it is installed or integrated
- Acceptance testing of the usability of a component may be done during component testing
- Acceptance testing of a new functional enhancement may come before system testing.

In iterative development, project teams can employ various forms of acceptance testing during and at the end of each iteration, or after a series of iterations, such as:

- Testing focused on verifying a new feature against its acceptance criteria
- Testing focused on validating that a new feature satisfies the users' needs
- Alpha tests and beta tests
- User acceptance tests, operational acceptance tests, regulatory acceptance tests, and contractual acceptance tests

Typical defects and failures

Examples of typical defects for any form of acceptance testing include:

- System workflows do not meet business or user requirements
- Business rules are not implemented correctly
- System does not satisfy contractual or regulatory requirements
- Non-functional failures such as security vulnerabilities, inadequate performance efficiency under high loads, or improper operation on a supported platform

Key exam take-out
• The purpose of **acceptance testing** is to validate the system is fit for purpose
• Performed by the potential or existing users of the system
• Conducted in a separate production like environment

2.3 Test types

A group of test activities can be aimed at verifying the software system (or a part of a system) based on a specific reason or target for testing.

A test type is focused on a particular test objective such as:

- Evaluating functional quality characteristics of the software such as completeness, correctness, and appropriateness **(Functional testing)**
- Evaluating non-functional quality characteristics, such as reliability, performance efficiency, security, compatibility, and usability **(Non-functional testing)**
- Evaluating the software structure/architecture (**White box testing**)
- Evaluating the effects of changes (**Change related testing**) i.e. confirming that defects have been fixed **(confirmation testing)** and looking for unintended changes **(regression testing)**

2.3.1 Functional Testing

Functional testing of a system involves tests that evaluate functions that the system should perform. It is the testing of "**what**" the system should do and can be unique to a system. For an airline website, user function can be search for a flight and book a flight. For an ATM software, the user functions can be check balance, withdraw cash, change pin.

Functional requirements may be described in work products such as:

- requirements specification
- use cases
- functional specification
- component specifications
- or they may be undocumented.

Functional tests should be **performed at all test levels** (e.g., tests for components may be based on a component specification), though the focus is different at each level.

Specification-based techniques may be used to derive test conditions and test cases from the functionality of the software or system. Functional testing considers the external behavior of the software i.e. its inputs and outputs, so black-box techniques may be used to derive test conditions and test cases for the functionality of the component or system (see chapter 4).

The thoroughness of functional testing can be measured through functional coverage.

Functional coverage (expressed as %) =

$$\frac{\text{Number of functional requirements exercised by tests}}{\text{Total number of functional requirements}} \times 100$$

For example, when using traceability between tests and functional requirements, the percentage of these requirements which are addressed by testing can be calculated. This can help in identifying coverage gaps.

Functional test design and execution may involve special skills or knowledge. It can be the knowledge of the particular business problem the software solves (e.g., payment software for the banking industry).

2.3.2 Non-functional testing

Non-functional testing evaluates software product quality characteristics of systems. These quality characteristics may relate to usability, reliability, portability, performance efficiency or security of the system. (Refer ISO standard (ISO/IEC 25010) for a classification of software product quality characteristics)

These tend to be generic requirements, which can be applied to many different systems. They will cover questions such as:

- How many concurrent users can the system support?
- How long is the data held locally before it is archived?
- How long will it take for a web-page to download?
- How many transactions can occur in a period of time?
- What is the maximum number of transactions that can take place?

Non-functional testing is the testing of "**how well**" the system behaves.

Non-functional testing may be performed at all test levels. Black-box techniques may be used to derive test conditions and test cases for non-functional testing. For example, boundary value analysis can be used to define the stress conditions for performance tests.

The thoroughness of non-functional testing can be measured through non-functional coverage.

Non-Functional coverage (expressed as %) =

$$\frac{\text{Number of non-functional requirements (of a type) exercised by tests}}{\text{Total number of non-functional requirements (of a type)}} \times 100$$

For example, using traceability between tests and supported devices for a mobile application, the percentage of devices which are addressed by compatibility testing can be calculated. This can help in identifying coverage gaps.

Non-functional test design and execution may involve special skills or knowledge, such as knowledge of the inherent weaknesses of a design or technology (e.g., security vulnerabilities associated with particular programming languages) or the particular user base (e.g., the personas of users of healthcare facility management systems).

> **Key exam take-out**
>
> Testing evaluates both functional and non-functional quality characteristics of the software.

2.3.3 White-box testing

White-box testing derives tests based on the system's internal structure or implementation. Internal structure may include code, architecture, work flows, and/or data flows within the system.

The thoroughness of white-box testing can be measured through structural coverage. Structural coverage is the extent to which some type of structural element has been exercised by tests and is expressed as a percentage of the type of element being covered.

At the component testing level, code coverage is based on the percentage of component code that has been tested and may be measured in terms of different aspects of code (coverage items) such as the percentage of executable statements tested in the component, or the percentage of decision outcomes tested. These types of coverage are collectively called code coverage. At the component integration testing level, white-box testing may be based on the architecture of the system, such as interfaces between components, and structural coverage may be measured in terms of the percentage of interfaces exercised by tests.

White-box test design and execution may involve special skills or knowledge, such as the way the code is built, how data is stored (e.g., to evaluate possible database queries), and how to use coverage tools and to correctly interpret their results.

2.3.4 Change-related testing

When changes are made to a system, either to correct a defect or because of new or changing functionality, testing should be done to confirm that the changes have corrected the defect or implemented the functionality correctly and have not caused any unforeseen adverse consequences.

- **Confirmation testing:** Once a defect has been found and fixed the software should be retested to confirm that the original defect has been successfully removed. This is called **confirmation testing**. This retesting may involve execution of all test cases that failed due to the defect. The software may also be tested to cover changes needed to fix the defect. In confirmation testing, the focus is on the changed area of software.

- **Regression testing:** It is a testing of existing software application to make sure that a change has not affected any existing functionality. The change can be made to the application code due to defect fix or for addition of any new functionality. This may also be due to change to the application environment, such as a new version of an operating system or database management system. These changes can have side-effects and may accidentally affect the behavior of other parts of the code, within the same component or in other components of the same system, or even in other systems. Regression testing involves running tests to detect such unintended side-effects.

Confirmation testing and regression testing are performed at all test levels.

In iterative and incremental development lifecycles (e.g., Agile), new features, changes to existing features, and code refactoring result in frequent changes to the code, which also requires change-related testing. Due to the evolving nature of the system, confirmation and regression testing are very important. This is particularly relevant for the Internet of Things (IOT) systems where individual objects (e.g., devices) are frequently updated or replaced.

Regression test suites are run many times and generally evolve slowly, so regression testing is a strong candidate for automation. Automation of these tests should start early in the project.

Key exam take-out

Confirmation testing confirms that the original defect has been successfully fixed; whereas **regression testing** confirms that the changes have not caused any side-effects.

2.3.5 Test Types and Test Levels

It is possible to perform any of the test types mentioned earlier at any test level. For a **banking application**, following examples show how functional, non-functional, white-box, and change-related tests will be used across all test levels.

The following are examples of functional tests:

- For component testing, tests are designed based on how a component should calculate compound interest.
- For component integration testing, tests are designed based on how account information captured at the user interface is passed to the business logic.
- For system testing, tests are designed based on how account holders can apply for a line of credit on their checking accounts.
- For system integration testing, tests are designed based on how the system uses an external microservice to check an account holder's credit score.
- For acceptance testing, tests are designed based on how the banker handles approving or declining a credit application.

The following are examples of non-functional tests:

- For component testing, performance tests are designed to evaluate the number of CPU cycles required to perform a complex total interest calculation.
- For component integration testing, security tests are designed for buffer overflow vulnerabilities due to data passed from the user interface to the business logic.
- For system testing, portability tests are designed to check whether the presentation layer works on all supported browsers and mobile devices.
- For system integration testing, reliability tests are designed to evaluate system robustness if the credit score microservice fails to respond.
- For acceptance testing, usability tests are designed to evaluate the accessibility of the banker's credit processing interface for people with disabilities.

The following are examples of white-box tests:

- For component testing, tests are designed to achieve complete statement and decision coverage for all components that perform financial calculations.
- For component integration testing, tests are designed to exercise how each screen in the browser interface passes data to the next screen and to the business logic.
- For system testing, tests are designed to cover sequences of web pages that can occur during a credit line application.
- For system integration testing, tests are designed to exercise all possible inquiry types sent to the credit score microservice.
- For acceptance testing, tests are designed to cover all supported financial data file structures and value ranges for bank-to-bank transfers.

Finally, the following are examples of change-related tests:

- For component testing, automated regression tests are built for each component and included within the continuous integration framework.
- For component integration testing, tests are designed to confirm fixes to interface-related defects as the fixes are checked into the code repository.
- For system testing, all tests for a given workflow are re-executed if any screen on that workflow changes.
- For system integration testing, tests of the application interacting with the credit scoring microservice are re-executed daily as part of continuous deployment of that microservice.
- For acceptance testing, all previously-failed tests are re-executed after a defect found in acceptance testing is fixed.

While this section provides examples of every test type across every level, it is not necessary, for all software, to have every test type represented across every level.

2.4 Maintenance testing

Once deployed to production environments, software and systems need to be maintained.

Changes to delivered software and systems are required due to:

- Fix defects discovered in operational use
- Add new functionality
- Delete existing functionality
- Modify already-delivered functionality
- Improve non-functional quality characteristics (e.g. performance efficiency, compatibility, reliability, security, and portability.)

When any changes are made to the system as part of maintenance, testing is performed to evaluate the success of the changes that were made and to check for any possible side-effects (e.g., regressions) in parts of the system that remain unchanged. This testing is called **maintenance testing**. Maintenance testing is required for both planned releases and unplanned releases (hot-fixes).

A maintenance release may require maintenance testing at multiple test levels, using various test types, based on its scope. The scope of maintenance testing depends on:

- The degree of risk of the change, for example, the degree to which the changed area of software communicates with other components or systems
- The size of the existing system
- The size of the change

2.4.1 Triggers for Maintenance

There are several reasons for having software maintenance and hence maintenance testing. These reasons can be for planned and unplanned changes.

Following are the triggers for maintenance testing:

Retirement:
- When an existing system reaches the end of its life and is retired from operation.
- This can require testing of **data migration or archiving** if long data-retention periods are required.

- Testing restores/retrieve procedures after archiving for long retention periods may also be needed.
- Regression testing may be needed to ensure that any functionality that remains in service still works.

Migration:
- **Migration from one platform to another** – This should include operational tests of the new environment as well as of the changed software. Examples: platform changes (PC to Mac), operating system changes (Windows to Unix)
- **Migration of data or data conversion** - Testing (conversion testing) is also needed when data from another application is migrated into the system being maintained.

Modifications:
- Planned enhancement or regular release changes
- Corrective changes
- Emergency changes
- Environment changes
- Database upgrades
- Upgrade of COTS software
- Patches for defects and vulnerability

For Internet of Things systems, maintenance testing may be triggered by the introduction of completely new or modified things, such as hardware devices and software services, into the overall system. The maintenance testing for such systems places particular emphasis on integration testing at different levels (e.g., network level, application level) and on security aspects, in particular, those relating to personal data.

Key exam take-out

The scope of maintenance testing is related to:
- Risk of the change
- Size of the existing system
- Complexity of the change.

2.4.2 Impact Analysis for Maintenance

Evaluating the expected consequences and possible side effects of a change on the existing system is called **impact analysis**.

It is used to identify:

- The expected consequences of a change
- Possible side effects of a change
- Areas in the system that will be affected by the change
- Impact of a change on existing tests
- Amount of regression testing required

After updating any existing tests affected by the change, regression testing is carried out on the side effects and affected areas in the system.

Impact analysis may be done **before a change is made**. This will help to decide if the change should be made, based on the potential consequences in other areas of the system.

Impact analysis can be difficult if:

- Specifications (e.g., business requirements, user stories, architecture) are out of date or missing
- Test cases are not documented or are out of date
- Bi-directional traceability between tests and the test basis has not been maintained
- Tool support is weak or non-existent
- The people involved do not have domain and/or system knowledge
- Insufficient attention has been paid to the software's maintainability during development

Key exam take-out
Impact analysis find out which areas of the system need to be tested for any change.

2.5 Relevant glossary terms and keywords

Glossary term	Definition
Alpha testing	Simulated or actual operational testing conducted in the developer's test environment, by roles outside the development organization.
Beta testing	Simulated or actual operational testing conducted at an external site, by roles outside the development organization.
Black box testing	Testing, either functional or non-functional, without reference to the internal structure of the component or system.
Change-related testing	A type of testing initiated by modification to a component or system.
Code coverage	An analysis method that determines which parts of the software have been executed (covered) by the test suite and which parts have not been executed, e.g. statement coverage, decision coverage or condition coverage.
Component testing	The testing of individual hardware or software components. [ISO 24765]
Component integration testing	Testing performed to expose defects in the interfaces and interactions between integrated components. [ISO 24765]
Confirmation testing	Dynamic testing conducted after fixing defects with the objective to confirm that failures caused by those defects do not occur anymore.
Commercial-Off-The-Shelf (COTS)	A software product that is developed for the general market, i.e. for a large number of customers, and that is delivered to many customers in identical format.
Contractual acceptance testing	Acceptance testing conducted to verify whether a system satisfies its contractual requirements.
Driver	A software component or test tool that replaces a component that takes care of the control and/or the calling of a component or system.
Functional requirement	A requirement that specifies a function that a component or system must be able to perform. [ISO 24765]
Functional testing	Testing conducted to evaluate the compliance of a component or system with functional requirements.

Glossary term	Definition
Impact analysis	The identification of all work products affected by a change, including an estimate of the resources needed to accomplish the change.
Integration	The process of combining components or systems into larger assemblies.
Integration testing	Testing performed to expose defects in the interfaces and in the interactions between integrated components or systems.
Interoperability testing	The process of testing to determine the interoperability of a software product.
Iterative-incremental development model	A development lifecycle where a project is broken into a usually large number of iterations. An iteration is a complete development loop resulting in a release (internal or external) of an executable product, a subset of the final product under development, which grows from iteration to iteration to become the final product.
Load testing	A type of performance testing conducted to evaluate the behavior of a component or system under varying loads, usually between anticipated conditions of low, typical, and peak usage.
Maintenance testing	Testing the changes to an operational system or the impact of a changed environment to an operational system.
Maintainability testing	The process of testing to determine the maintainability of a software product.
Non-functional testing	Testing conducted to evaluate the compliance of a component or system with non-functional requirements.
Operational acceptance testing	Operational testing in the acceptance test phase, typically performed in a (simulated) operational environment by operations and/or systems administration staff focusing on operational aspects, e.g., recoverability, resource-behavior, installability and technical compliance.
Performance testing	The process of testing to determine the performance of a software product.
Portability testing	The process of testing to determine the portability of a software product.

Glossary term	Definition
Regression testing	A type of change-related testing to detect whether defects have been introduced or uncovered in unchanged areas of the software.
Regulatory acceptance testing	A type of acceptance testing performed to verify whether a system conforms to relevant laws, policies and regulations.
Robustness testing	Testing to determine the robustness of the software product. Robustness is defined as the degree to which a component or system can function correctly in the presence of invalid inputs or stressful environmental conditions.
Reliability testing	Testing to determine the reliability of a software product. Reliability is defined as the degree to which a component or system performs specified functions under specified conditions for a specified period of time.
Security testing	Testing to determine the security of the software product. Security is defined as the degree to which a component or system protects information and data so that persons or other components or systems have the degree of access appropriate to their types and levels of authorization.
Sequential development model	A type of development lifecycle model in which a complete system is developed in a linear way of several discrete and successive phases with no overlap between them.
Stress testing	A type of performance testing conducted to evaluate a system or component at or beyond the limits of its anticipated or specified work loads, or with reduced availability of resources such as access to memory or servers [ISO 24765]
Stub	A skeletal or special-purpose implementation of a software component used to develop or test a component that calls or is otherwise dependent on it. It replaces a called component. [IEEE 610]
System integration testing	A test level that focuses on interactions between systems.
System testing	A test level that focuses on verifying that a system as a whole meets specified requirements.

Glossary term	Definition
Test basis	The body of knowledge used as the basis for test analysis and design.
Test environment	An environment containing hardware, instrumentation, simulators, software tools, and other support elements needed to conduct a test. [After ISO 24765]
Test level	A specific instantiation of a test process.
Test object	The work product to be tested.
Test objective	The reason or purpose of testing.
Test type	A group of test activities based on specific test objectives aimed at specific characteristics of a component or system
Test-driven development	A software development technique in which the test cases are developed, and often automated, and then the software is developed incrementally to pass those test cases.
Usability testing	Testing to evaluate the degree to which the system can be used by specified users with effectiveness, efficiency and satisfaction in a specified context of use. [ISO 25010]
User acceptance testing	A type of acceptance testing performed to determine if intended users accept the system.
Validation	Confirmation by examination and through provision of objective evidence that the requirements for a specific intended use or application have been fulfilled. [ISO 9000]
Verification	Confirmation by examination and through provision of objective evidence that specified requirements have been fulfilled. [ISO 9000]
V-model	A sequential development lifecycle model describing a one-for-one relationship between major phases of software development from business requirements specification to delivery, and corresponding test levels from acceptance testing to component testing.
White-box testing	Testing based on an analysis of the internal structure of the component or system.

2.6 Quiz

Question 1

"Finding defects" is NOT the main objective for which of the following test level?

a) Component testing
b) Integration testing
c) System testing
d) Acceptance testing.

Question 2

Which of the following statements BEST describes the Incremental software development model?

a) Design, build and testing activities are often overlapping throughout the overall development cycle.
b) The testing activities start once the development activities are completed.
c) Each cycle delivers a working software which is a subset of the overall set of features.
d) Specifying requirements, design, build and testing are done in a series with added pieces.

Question 3

Which of the following work products (1-4) are commonly used as a test basis for the different level of testing (A-D)?

1. Legal contracts
2. Code
3. Sequence diagrams
4. Non-functional requirements

A. Component testing
B. Integration testing
C. System testing
D. Acceptance testing

a) 1D, 2A, 3B, 4C.
b) 1D, 2B, 3A, 4C.
c) 1C, 2D, 3B, 4A.
d) 1A, 2C, 3D, 4B.

Question 4

Which of the following is TRUE in relation to alpha and beta testing?

I. Beta testing is performed at the developing organization's site
II. Beta testing is performed by Independent testers
III. Alpha testing is performed at the developing organization's site
IV. Alpha testing is performed by the developer

a) II & III
b) III & IV
c) I & IV
d) only III

Question 5

Which of the following is required for change-related test design and execution?

a) Knowledge of the inherent drawbacks of design or technology.
b) Knowledge of changes made to the system.
c) Knowledge of how the code is built and how the data is stored.
d) Knowledge of the business domain of the system.

Question 6

Which of the following TWO can affect the scope of maintenance testing?

a) The size of the change
b) The number of regression test cases to be executed
c) The size of the existing system.
d) The number of test levels

Question 7

For the maintenance testing in the project, which of the following conditions will LEAST likely make the impact analysis task difficult?

a) The test data used for testing is not available.
b) There is no traceability between test cases and requirement.
c) The test cases for regression testing are out of date.
d) The people involved in impact analysis are new to the project.

2.7 Answers

1	2	3	4	5	6	7
D	D	A	D	B	A, C	A

Question 1

FL-2.2.1 (K2) Compare the different test levels from the perspective of objectives, test basis, test objects, typical defects and failures, and approaches and responsibilities

Justification

a) Not correct - Finding defects is one of the main objectives of Component testing.
b) Not correct - Finding defects is one of the main objectives of Integration testing.
c) Not correct - Finding defects is one of the main objectives of System testing.
d) **Correct** - Finding defects is NOT the main objectives of Acceptance testing. If there are a significant number of defects found during acceptance testing may in some cases be considered a major project risk. (Syllabus 2.2.4)

Question 2

FL-2.1.1 (K2) Explain the relationship between software development activities and test activities in the software life cycle

Justification

a) Not correct - This describes the **Iterative model**. Syllabus 2.1.1
b) Not correct - This describes the **waterfall model** (sequential development). Syllabus 2.1.1
c) Not correct - This describes the **Iterative model**. Syllabus 2.1.1
d) **Correct** - This is related to the **Incremental model**. Syllabus 2.1.1

Question 3

FL-2.2.1 (K2) Compare the different test levels from the perspective of objectives, test basis, test objects, typical defects and failures, and approaches and responsibilities

Justification

- **Legal contracts** are typical work products used as test basis for **acceptance testing**. Syllabus 2.2.4. **(1D)**
- **Code** is a typical work product used as test basis for **component testing**. Syllabus 2.2.1. **(2A)**
- **Sequence diagrams** are typical work products used as test basis for **integration testing**. Syllabus 2.2.2. **(3B)**
- **Non-Functional requirements** are typical work products used as test basis for **system testing**. Syllabus 2.2.3. **(4C)**

Thus:

a) **Correct**
b) Not correct
c) Not correct
d) Not correct

Question 4

FL-2.2.1 (K2) Compare the different test levels from the perspective of objectives, test basis, test objects, typical defects and failures, and approaches and responsibilities

Justification

- This is False, Beta testing is performed at the customer's site. (Syllabus 2.2.4)
- This is False, Beta testing is performed by potential or existing customer's and not by independent testers. (Syllabus 2.2.4)
- This is True, Alpha testing is performed at developing organization site. (Syllabus 2.2.4)
- This is False, Alpha testing is performed by potential or existing customer's and not by developers. (Syllabus 2.2.4)

Thus:

a) Not correct
b) Not correct
c) Not correct
d) **Correct**

Question 5

FL-2.3.1 (K2) Compare functional, non-functional, and white-box testing

Justification

a) Not correct – For **Non-functional** test design and execution knowledge of the inherent drawbacks of design or technology is required. (Syllabus 2.3.2)
b) **Correct** -For **change-related** test design and execution thorough knowledge of changes made to the system is required. (Syllabus 2.3.4)
c) Not correct - For **White-box** test design and execution knowledge of the way the code is built and how data is stored is required. (Syllabus 2.3.3)
d) Not correct -For **Functional test** design and execution knowledge of the business, domain is required. (Syllabus 2.3.1)

Question 6

FL-2.4.1 (K2) Summarize triggers for maintenance testing

Justification

a) **Correct** – The size of the change can affect the scope of maintenance testing. (Syllabus 2.4.1).
b) Not correct – The number of test cases to be executed will be decided based on the scope of maintenance testing. (Syllabus 2.4.1).
c) **Correct** – The size of the existing system can affect the scope of maintenance testing. (Syllabus 2.4.1).
d) Not correct – The number of the test levels will be decided based on the scope of maintenance testing. (Syllabus 2.4.1).

Question 7

FL-2.4.2 (K2) Describe the role of impact analysis in maintenance testing

Justification

a) **Correct** – This will make the actual maintenance testing difficult not the impact analysis task.
b) Not correct - If the traceability between tests and test basis is not maintained it can make the impact analysis task difficult. Syllabus 2.4.2
c) Not correct - If the test cases for regression testing are out of date it can make the impact analysis task difficult. Syllabus 2.4.2
d) Not correct - If the people involved in impact analysis are new to the project or do not possess domain knowledge it can make the impact analysis task difficult. Syllabus 2.4.2

3 Static Testing

Learning objective for Static Testing 88
3.1 Static testing basics 89
    3.1.1 Work Products that Can Be Examined by Static Testing 89
    3.1.2 Benefits of Static Testing 90
    3.1.3 Difference between Static and Dynamic Testing 91
3.2 Review process 93
    3.2.1 Work Product Review process 93
    3.2.2 Roles and responsibilities in a formal review 95
    3.2.3 Review Types 96
    3.2.4 Applying Review Techniques 101
    3.2.5 Success Factors for Reviews 104
3.3 Relevant glossary terms and keywords 106
3.4 Quiz 108
3.5 Answers 111

Learning objective for Static Testing

Following learning objectives are covered in this chapter:

3.1 Static Testing Basics

FL-3.1.1 (K1) Recognize types of software work product that can be examined by the different static testing techniques

FL-3.1.2 (K2) Use examples to describe the value of static testing

FL-3.1.3 (K2) Explain the difference between static and dynamic techniques, considering objectives, types of defects to be identified, and the role of these techniques within the software lifecycle

3.2 Review Process

FL-3.2.1 (K2) Summarize the activities of the work product review process

FL-3.2.2 (K1) Recognize the different roles and responsibilities in a formal review

FL-3.2.3 (K2) Explain the differences between different review types: informal review, walkthrough, technical review, and inspection

FL-3.2.4 (K3) Apply a review technique to work product to find defects

FL-3.2.5 (K2) Explain the factors that contribute to a successful review

3.1 Static testing basics

Historically testing was limited to dynamic test techniques, where testing is performed only after the code is executed. In contrast to dynamic testing, static testing can be performed without executing the code. It can be performed on any work product used in the software development lifecycle.

Static testing can be divided into two categories:

- **Reviews** - manual examination of work products
- **Static Analysis** - Tool-driven evaluation of the code or any other work products

Static analysis is important for:

- **Safety-critical computer systems** - Systems used in aviation, medical, or nuclear software are highly complex and require a high level of code coverage which is possible only with static analysis tools.
- **Security testing** - Static analysis tools look for a fixed set of patterns, or rules, in the code which is more vulnerable to security attacks. A new set of patterns can be easily added to enhance the capability of these tools.
- **Continuous delivery/continuous deployment** - Static analysis is part of the automated software build and distribution tools that are used in Agile development.

Key exam take-out

Both categories of static testing (reviews/static analysis) can assess the code or other work product being tested without actually executing the code or work product being tested.

3.1.1 Work Products that Can Be Examined by Static Testing

Virtually any work product produced during the software development lifecycle can be reviewed. These includes:

- **Specifications work products** – Functional requirements documents, business requirements, and security requirements
- **Business-oriented work products used in Agile projects** - Epics, user stories, and acceptance criteria

- **Design work products** - Architecture documents, data specifications software, and hardware design specifications
- **Development work products** – Code, automated and manual unit test cases
- **Testing work products** - Test strategies, test plans, manual and automated test cases, and any other test documentation
- **Project work products** - Project plans, resource plans, contracts, project plans, schedules, and budget planning
- **User work products** - User manuals, web pages, help guides
- **System admin work products** - Configuration set-up and infrastructure set-up guides/manuals
- **Models** – Data models and activity diagrams

Reviews can be applied to any work product that the participants can read and understand.

Static analysis can be applied to any work product with a formal structure (typically code or models) for which an appropriate static analysis tool exists. Static analysis can even be applied with tools that evaluate work products written in natural language such as requirement documents for spelling errors, grammatical mistakes, and readability.

3.1.2 Benefits of Static Testing

A major benefit of static testing, when applied early in the software development lifecycle, is that defects are detected before dynamic testing is performed. These defects are often much cheaper to remove than those detected while running tests.

For example, a defect, in the requirements specification may propagate itself to the design, the code, and even the test cases. The sooner a defect is found and corrected the better. If the defect is not detected and fixed at the point of introduction the cost of fixing it increases for each further phase achieved in the software development lifecycle. However, the actual cost will depend on multiple factors such as individual project, staff, process, procedures, types of applications, etc. Therefore, it is always cheaper and easier to fix the defect the earlier it is found in project.

The static testing is a very effective way of reducing the overall costs of development by:

Early defect detection and correction

Defects found earlier in the development life cycle, such as those found in requirements, are often much cheaper to remove than those detected by running tests by executing code. This is because there is a smaller correction loop involved when it is found earlier.

Development productivity improvements

By reviewing the system documentation, errors can be driven out before coding begins. The developers will receive higher-quality documentation and therefore are likely to produce higher-quality code.

Reduced development timescales

Less rework required due to good quality understandable documentation, developers can be more productive and coding can be achieved quicker.

Testing time and cost reductions

Higher-quality code delivered to the testers from development reduces the cost of testing. This is because there will be few defects which will result in fewer retest cycles and less development effort for re-coding/re-design.

Lifetime cost reductions

The software which has fewer defects in the live production environment has a lower lifetime cost because of the reduced levels of operational support and maintenance required.

Fewer defects

Defects are manifestations of errors in the code. A good review process eliminates many of the errors and so levels of defects found will be reduced.

Improved communication

Reviews are a way to pass on information as much as they are about finding issues in the item under review. By involving the correct people in reviews, details of the system are being passed on at the earliest stage of the software development life cycle. The review process also opens a dialogue between different team members within a project.

It is estimated that on-going review costs only about **15% of the development budget** but can uncover **70% of the project issues** during the review process.

3.1.3 Difference between Static and Dynamic Testing

Static testing and dynamic testing can have the same objectives such as providing an assessment of the quality of the work products and identifying defects as early as possible. Static and dynamic testing complement each other by finding different types of defects.

One main distinction is that static testing finds defects in work products directly rather than identifying failures caused by defects when the software is run. A defect can reside in a work product for a very long time without causing a failure. The path where the defect lies may be rarely exercised or hard to reach, so it will not be easy to construct and execute a dynamic test that encounters it. Static testing may be able to find the defect with much less effort.

Another distinction is that static testing can be used to improve the consistency and internal quality of work products, while dynamic testing typically focuses on externally visible behavior.

Compared with dynamic testing, typical defects that are easier and cheaper to find and fix through static testing include:

- **Requirement defects** - Inconsistencies, ambiguities, contradictions, omissions, inaccuracies, and redundancies
- **Design defects** - Inefficient algorithms or database structures, high coupling, low cohesion
- **Coding defects** - Variables with undefined values, variables that are declared but never used, unreachable code, duplicate code
- **Deviations from standards** - Lack of adherence to coding standards
- **Incorrect interface specifications** - Different units of measurement/ different variable types in the integrated interfaces
- **Security vulnerabilities** - Susceptibility to buffer overflows
- **Gaps or inaccuracies in test basis traceability or coverage** - Missing tests for an acceptance criterion

Moreover, most types of maintainability defects can only be found by static testing such as:

- Improper modularization
- Poor reusability of components
- Code that is difficult to analyze
- Code that is difficult to modify without introducing new defects

3.2 Review process

Reviews vary from informal to formal. **Informal reviews** are characterized by not following a defined process and not having formally documented output. **Formal reviews are** characterized by team participation, documented results of the review, and documented procedures for conducting the review.

The formality of a review process is related to factors such as

- Software development lifecycle model
- Maturity of the development process
- The complexity of the work product to be reviewed
- Legal or regulatory requirements
- The need for an audit trail

The focus of a review depends on the agreed objectives of the review such as

- Finding defects
- Gaining understanding
- Educating participants such as testers and new team members
- Discussing and deciding by consensus

More details of the review process for work products, including roles and review techniques can be found in ISO standard (ISO/IEC 20246).

3.2.1 Work Product Review process

The review process comprises the following main activities:

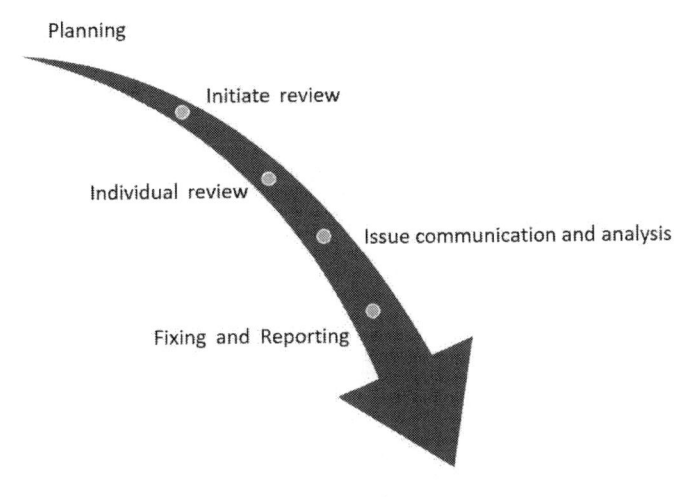

- Planning
- Initiate review
- Individual review
- Issue communication and analysis
- Fixing and Reporting

Work Product Review process

Planning

- Defining the scope, which includes the purpose of the review, what documents or parts of documents to review, and the quality characteristics to be evaluated
- Estimating effort and timeframe
- Identifying review characteristics such as the review type with roles, activities, and checklists
- Selecting the people to participate in the review and allocating roles
- Defining the entry and exit criteria for more formal review types (e.g., inspections)
- Checking that entry criteria are met (for more formal review types)

Initiate review

- Distributing the work product (physically or by electronic means) and other material, such as issue log forms, checklists, and related work products
- Explaining the scope, objectives, process, roles, and work products to the participants
- Answering any questions that participants may have about the review

Individual review (i.e. individual preparation)

- Reviewing all or part of the work product
- Noting potential defects, recommendations, and questions

Issue communication and analysis

- Communicating identified potential defects (e.g., in a review meeting)
- Analyzing potential defects, assigning ownership and status to them
- Evaluating and documenting quality characteristics
- Evaluating the review findings against the exit criteria to make a review decision (reject; major changes needed; accept, possibly with minor changes)

Fixing and reporting

- Creating defect reports for those findings that require changes to a work product
- Fixing defects found (typically done by the author) in the work product reviewed

- Communicating defects to the appropriate person or team (when found in a work product related to the work product reviewed)
- Recording updated status of defects (in formal reviews), potentially including the agreement of the comment originator
- Gathering metrics (for more formal review types)
- Checking that exit criteria are met (for more formal review types)
- Accepting the work product when the exit criteria are reached

3.2.2 Roles and responsibilities in a formal review

A typical inspection or other formal review is likely to include the roles below:

Author

- Creates the work product under review
- Fixes defects in the work product under review (if necessary)

Management

- Is responsible for review planning
- Decides on the execution of reviews
- Assigns staff, budget, and time
- Monitors ongoing cost-effectiveness
- Executes control decisions in the event of inadequate outcomes

Facilitator (Moderator)

- Ensures effective running of review meetings (when held)
- Mediates, if necessary, between the various points of view
- Is often the person upon whom the success of the review depends

Review Leader

- Takes overall responsibility for the review
- Decides who will be involved and organizes when and where it will take place

Reviewers

- May be subject matter experts, persons working on the project, stakeholders with an interest in the work product, and/or individuals with specific technical or business backgrounds
- Identify potential defects in the work product under review

- May represent different perspectives (e.g., tester, developer, user, operator, business analyst, usability expert, etc.)

Scribe (recorder)

- Collates potential defects found during the individual review activity
- Records new potential defects, open points, and decisions from the review meeting (when held)

In some review types, one person may play more than one role, and the actions associated with each role may also vary based on review type. When the tools are used to support the review process, especially in the logging of defects, open points, and decisions, there is often no need for a scribe.

ISO standard (ISO/IEC 20246) provides more details on the roles.

3.2.3 Review Types

Reviews can be used for various purposes but one of the main objectives is to **find defects**.

Some of the common selection criteria for selecting a review type are:

- Needs of the project
- Available resources
- Product Type
- Product risks
- Business domain
- Company culture

A single work product may be the subject of more than one review. If more than one type of review is used, the order may vary. For example, an informal review may be carried out before a technical review, or inspection may be carried out on a requirement specification before a walkthrough with customers.

The types of reviews described below can be done as peer reviews, i.e., done by colleagues qualified to do the same work.

The types of defects found in a review vary, depending especially on the work product being reviewed.

Reviews can be classified according to various attributes. These attributes are characterized by the level of documentation, entry and exit criteria, process and rules pertaining to the review.

Following are the most common types of reviews:

- Informal review
- Walkthrough
- Technical review
- Inspection.

Informal review (e.g., buddy check, pairing, pair review)

Informal reviews have **no formal process defined** and may be as simple as a programmer reviewing other developer's code or a tester reviewing other tester's test cases, or two team members working together so the development and review of the work product happen simultaneously.

Documentation of the review is not mandated but is sometimes produced.

The main purpose of an informal review is to find defects. It usually requires little investment, due to the lack of any formal process being required, but can be effective, depending on the skills and motivation of the reviewer.

Following are the main characteristics of Informal review:

- **Main purpose**: detecting potential defects
- **Possible additional purposes**: generating new ideas or solutions, quickly solving minor problems
- Not based on a formal (documented) process
- May not involve a review meeting
- May be performed by a colleague of the author (buddy check) or by more people
- Results may be documented
- Varies in usefulness depending on the reviewers
- Use of checklists is optional
- Very commonly used in Agile development

Key exam take-out
Informal review- No meeting or facilitator requirement

Walkthrough

Walkthroughs are typically used to check early drafts of work products. For instance, in the case of a new design, a walkthrough can allow a peer group to gain a better understanding of the approach being taken in the design. In return, those in attendance can offer their guidance on the process.

Following are the main characteristics of the walkthrough:

- **Main purposes**: find defects, improve the software product, consider alternative implementations, evaluate conformance to standards and specifications
- **Possible additional purposes**: exchanging ideas about techniques or style variations, training of participants, achieving consensus
- Individual preparation before the review meeting is optional
- The review meeting is typically led by the author of the work product
- Scribe is mandatory
- Use of checklists is optional
- May take the form of scenarios, dry runs, or simulations
- Potential defect logs and review reports are produced
- May vary in practice from quite informal to very formal

Key exam take-out

Walkthrough- The main purpose is to find defects and gain understanding or learn about the work product.

Technical review

A technical review has a well-defined process, generating records of errors found and actions to be taken. The review meeting is conducted as a formal meeting, with a defined facilitator (who must not be the author). This person is ideally trained in conducting reviews.

Reviewers have technical expertise in their disciplines, relevant to the work product being reviewed.

Pre-meeting preparation is essential for a formal review and typically checklists are used and a report prepared, though these aspects are not mandatory.

A technical review is usually conducted to do one or more of the following: discuss, make decisions, evaluate alternatives, find defects, solve technical problems or check conformance to specifications and standards.

Following are the main characteristics of technical review:

- **Main purposes**: gaining consensus, detecting potential defects
- **Possible further purposes**: evaluating the quality and building confidence in the work product, generating new ideas, motivating and enabling authors to improve future work products, considering alternative implementations
- Reviewers should be technical peers of the author and technical experts in the same or other disciplines
- Individual preparation before the review meeting is required
- Review meeting is optional, ideally led by a trained facilitator (typically not the author)
- Scribe is mandatory, ideally not the author
- Use of checklists is optional
- Potential defect logs and review reports are produced

Key exam take-out

Technical review - A well-defined process focuses on finding defects and evaluating the quality **of technical work product.** Reviewers have technical expertise relevant to work product.

Inspection

Inspections are the most formal type of reviews and focus on a particular work product. They were introduced at IBM in the early 1970s by Michael Fagan and have been praised as one of the single most significant process changes.

Inspections require a trained moderator, who should not be the author and all other roles are defined before the inspection.

Inspections follow a formal process based on rules and checklists and the process includes entry and exit criteria. Metrics are collected and used to improve processes as well as documents.

Pre-meeting preparation is essential and an inspection report with a list of findings is a mandatory component, as is a formal follow-up process.

The main purpose of an inspection is to find defects, but the process can also be used for initiating process improvements based on the metrics that are gathered.

Following are the main characteristics of inspection:

- **Main purposes**: detecting potential defects, evaluating the quality and building confidence in the work product, preventing future similar defects through author learning and root cause analysis
- **Possible further purposes**: motivating and enabling authors to improve future work products and the software development process, achieving consensus
- Follows a defined process with formally documented outputs, based on rules and checklists
- Uses clearly defined roles, which are mandatory, and may include a dedicated reader (who reads the work product aloud often paraphrase, i.e. describing it in own words, during the review meeting)
- Individual preparation before the review meeting is required
- Reviewers are either peer of the author or experts in other disciplines that are relevant to the work product
- Specified entry and exit criteria are used
- Scribe is mandatory
- The review meeting is led by a trained facilitator (not the author)
- The author cannot act as the review leader, reader, or scribe
- Potential defect logs and review report are produced
- Metrics are collected and used to improve the entire software development process, including the inspection process

---

Key exam take-out

Inspection - A formal review process based on rules and checklists and specified entry and exit criteria for acceptance of the work product.

Useful for work products related to safety-critical applications.

Static Testing | 101

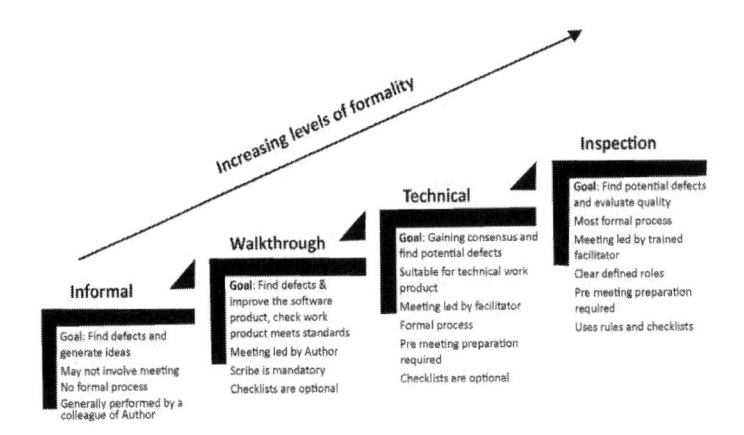

```
                                                        Inspection
                                    Increasing levels of formality
                                                        Goal: Find potential defects
                                                        and evaluate quality
                                        Technical       Most formal process
                                                        Meeting led by trained
                            Walkthrough  Goal: Gaining consensus and  facilitator
                                         find potential defects
                                                        Clear defined roles
                            Goal: Find defects &  Suitable for technical work
                Informal    improve the software  product  Pre meeting preparation
                            product, check work   Meeting led by facilitator  required
                            product meets standards
    Goal: Find defects and                         Formal process  Uses rules and checklists
    generate ideas          Meeting led by Author  Pre meeting preparation
    May not involve meeting Scribe is mandatory    required
    No formal process       Checklists are optional Checklists are optional
    Generally performed by a
    colleague of Author
```

Different Review Types

3.2.4 Applying Review Techniques

There are a number of review techniques that can be applied during the individual review (i.e., individual preparation) activity to uncover defects. These techniques can be used across the review types described above. The effectiveness of the techniques may differ depending on the type of review used. Examples of different individual review techniques for various review types are listed below.

Ad hoc

- In an ad hoc review, reviewers are provided with little or no guidance on how this task should be performed.
- Reviewers often read the work product sequentially, identifying and documenting issues as they encounter them.
- **Example**: Different reviewers irrespective of their background or experience can be asked to go through a work product to find out any obvious issues such as ambiguous statements or missing information.
- **Advantage**: This is a commonly used technique which requires little or no preparation.
- **Risk**: This technique is highly dependent on reviewer skills and may lead to many duplicate issues being reported by different reviewers.

Checklist-based

- A checklist-based review is a systematic technique, whereby the reviewers detect issues based on **checklists** that are distributed during the review initiation, generally, by the facilitator.
- A review checklist consists of a set of questions based on potential defects, which may be derived from experience.
- Checklists should be specific to the type of work product under review and should be maintained regularly to cover issue types missed in previous reviews.
- **Example**: Consider a list of potential defects which are compiled based on experience or results from previous reviews. Reviewers can use this list as a checklist to find similar errors in the work product under review.
- **Advantage**: This technique provides systematic coverage of typical defect types.
- **Risk**: Reviewers can simply focus on the checklist and can miss other defects. If the checklists are outdated the review won't be effective. It is therefore recommended for reviewers to look for defects outside the checklist rather than simply follow the checklist. Also, the checklists should be up to date.

Scenarios and dry runs

- In a scenario-based review, reviewers are provided with structured guidelines on how to read through the work product.
- A scenario-based review supports reviewers in performing "dry runs" on the work product based on the expected usage of the work product.
- **Example**: Consider a work product which is describing requirements in the form of use cases. Reviewers can review this work product to validate the content and to make sure it is documented in a suitable use case format.
- **Advantage**: These scenarios provide reviewers with better guidelines on how to identify specific defect types than simple checklist entries.
- **Risk**: As with checklist-based reviews, reviewers could be constrained to the documented scenarios. It is therefore recommended for reviewers to look for other defect types (e.g., missing features) which are outside the documented scenarios.

Perspective-based

- In perspective-based reading, similar to a role-based review, reviewers take on different stakeholder viewpoints during individual reviewing.
- Typical stakeholder viewpoints can include end-user, marketing, designer, tester, or operations.
- Using different stakeholder viewpoints leads to more depth in individual reviewing with less duplication of issues across reviewers.
- Perspective-based reading also requires the reviewers to attempt to use the work product under review to generate the product they would derive from it.
- To increase the effectiveness of perspective-based reading, checklists are expected to be used.
- **Example**: A tester would attempt to generate draft acceptance tests if performing a perspective-based reading on a requirements specification to see if all the necessary information was included.
- **Advantage**: Empirical studies have shown perspective-based reading to be the most effective general technique for reviewing requirements and technical work products.
- **Risk**: For this technique to be effective, it is important to include and weight different stakeholder viewpoints appropriately, based on risks.

Role-based

- A role-based review is a technique in which the reviewers evaluate the work product from the perspective of individual stakeholder roles. The same principles apply as in perspective-based reading because the roles are similar.
- Typical roles include specific end-user types (experienced, inexperienced, senior, child, etc.), and specific roles in the organization (user administrator, system administrator, performance tester, etc.).
- **Example**: Consider a configuration work product which covers the authorization, privilege and security attributes for different system users. i.e. Primary admin (super-user), System Admin, Operator. Different reviewers will be assigned a particular role. They will then review the work product for the perspective of that role to find out if the authorization, privilege and security attributes are defined correctly for that particular role in the work product.
- **Advantage**: Role-based review help to uncover many defects which are related to the use of work product based on the particular user role. It also helps to explore the work product based on a particular user role.
- **Risk**: The reviewers who are playing a particular role should have a good understanding of the role and their functions.

> **Exercise:**
>
> The design workflow of a customer service system is under review. This system allows three different types of users to access the system based on the access permissions.
>
> "Level-1" users can access all the customer information but if they make any changes to customer personal information it goes to the "Level-2" users' workflow for approval. If they make any changes to customer financial information, it goes to Manager user's workflow for approval. Users with "Level-2" or "Manager" access can review this information respectively and can approve or reject the changes.
>
> The team is considering using different review techniques to verify the design workflow. Which of the review technique will be MOST suitable for this situation?
>
> a) Scenarios and dry runs
> b) Checklist-based
> c) Role-based
> d) Ad hoc
>
> As there are different user roles for this system (Level-1, Level-2, Manager). Therefore, the **role-based review technique** will be most suitable to cover the design from the perspective of the end-users of the system.

3.2.5 Success Factors for Reviews

There are a number of factors that are required to have a successful review.

Organizational success factors for reviews include:

- **Clear Objectives** – During the review meeting review objective should be defined. It should be clear and tangible so it can be used as measurable exit criteria.
- **Selecting appropriate Review Type** – Review type should be selected which are suitable to achieve the objectives and are appropriate to the type and level of software work products and participants
- **Use of checklists and roles** – Checklist-based or role-based reviewing are suitable to effectively find defects in the work product irrespective of any review techniques used. The checklists used should address the main risks and should be up to date.

- **Small work products for review** – Large documents should be written and reviewed in small chunks, this will help to provide authors early and frequent feedback on defects.
- **Adequate time and notice** – Participants should be given adequate time and notice for the preparation.
- **Management support** – There should be adequate time incorporating for review activities in the schedules.
- **Company quality policy** – Reviews should be integrated in the company's quality and/or test policies.

People-related success factors for reviews include:
- **Right participants** -The right set of people should be involved to meet the review objectives, for example, people with different skill sets or perspectives, who may use the document as a work input.
- **Testers as reviewers** - Testers should be seen as valued reviewers who can contribute to the review and learn about the work product. This would also enable them to prepare more effective tests and to prepare those tests earlier.
- **Well-managed process** - The whole review process should be well managed. Reviews are conducted on small chunks so that reviewers do not lose focus during individual review and/or during the review meeting. The meeting is well-managed so that participants consider it a valuable use of their time and dedicate adequate time and attention to detail.
- **A learning environment where defects are welcomed** - A culture of learning and process improvement is promoted when defects found are acknowledged, appreciated, and handled objectively.
- **Atmosphere of trust** - The review is conducted in an environment where the outcome is not used for the evaluation of the participants. Also, participants should avoid any behaviors that might indicate hostility to other participants.
- **Training needs** - Some of the formal review types such as inspections need adequate training for participants. These training sessions should be conducted prior to the reviews.

3.3 Relevant glossary terms and keywords

Glossary term	Definition
Ad hoc review	A review technique performed informally without a structured process.
Checklist-based review	A review technique guided by a list of questions or required attributes.
Dynamic testing	Testing that involves the execution of the software of a component or system.
Entry criteria	The set of conditions for officially starting a defined task
Exit criteria	The set of conditions for officially completing a defined task.
Formal review	A type of review that follows a defined process with a formally documented output.
Informal review	A type of review without a formal (documented) procedure.
Inspection	A type of formal review to identify issues in a work product, which provides measurement to improve the review process and the software development process. [ISO 20246]
Metric	A measurement scale and the method used for measurement.
Moderator/ Facilitator	The person responsible for running review meetings
Perspective-based reading	A review technique in which a work product is evaluated from the perspective of different stakeholders with the purpose to derive other work products.
Technical review	A type of formal review by a team of technically-qualified personnel that examines the quality of a work product and identifies discrepancies from specifications and standards
Reviewer	A participant in a review, who identifies issues in the work product.
Review	A type of static testing in which a work product or process is evaluated by one or more individuals to detect defects or to provide improvements.
Role-based review	A review technique in which a work product is evaluated from the perspective of different stakeholders.

Glossary term	Definition
Scribe / Recorder	A person who records information during the review meetings.
Scenario-based review	A review technique in which a work product is evaluated to determine its ability to address specific scenarios.
Static analysis	The process of evaluating a component or system without executing it, based on its form, structure, content, or documentation.
Static testing	Testing a work product without code being executed.
Walkthrough	A type of review in which an author leads members of the review through a work product and the members ask questions and make comments about possible issues.

3.4 Quiz

Question 1

Which of the following statement describing the difference between static and dynamic testing is TRUE?

a) The objective of static testing is to provide an assessment of the quality of the work product whereas dynamic testing provides an assessment of the quantity of the work product.
b) The objective of static testing is to find defects, whereas the objective of dynamic testing is to find failures.
c) Dynamic testing can find the similar defects found during static testing but with much less effort.
d) Static testing focuses on improving the internal quality of the work products, whereas dynamic testing typically focuses on externally visible behaviors.

Question 2

Which of the following TWO statements about static testing are true?

a) Static testing helps in validating the requirements early in the lifecycle.
b) Static testing decreases the development cost but increases the testing cost.
c) Static testing increases development productivity.
d) Static testing can find run-time issues before dynamic testing.

Question 3

Which of the following review type is BEST suited for review of a design document for a safety-critical system?

a) Technical Review.
b) Informal Review.
c) Inspection.
d) Walkthrough.

Question 4

In the formal review, who is primarily responsible for executing control decisions in the event of inadequate outcomes during the review activity?

a) Facilitator
b) Reviewers
c) Author
d) Management

Question 5

In which phase of a work product review process the scope, objectives, process, role, and work products are explained to the participants?

a) Planning
b) Initiate review
c) Individual review
d) Issue communication and analysis.

Question 6

A team is using perspective-based review techniques to review the use-cases for the ATM system. This user can perform functions as shown in the following use case diagram. For the reviewer who has taken the role of "end-user", which of the following will be appropriate to check the effectiveness of the work-product?

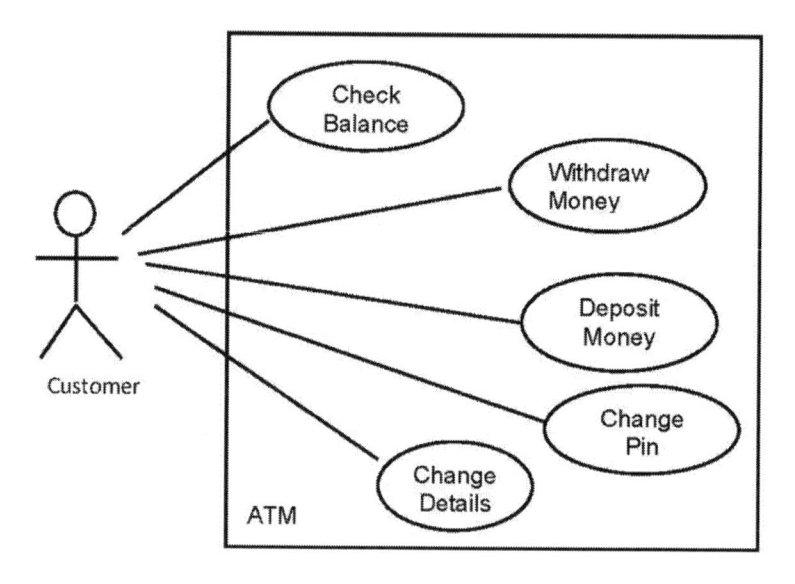

a) Find as many defects in the work product from an end user's perspective.
b) Check the work product sequentially and identify and document issues as they encounter them.
c) Generate a draft of acceptance test cases using the work product.
d) Find the issues in the work product based on the potential defects list.

3.5 Answers

1	2	3	4	5	6
D	A, C	C	D	B	C

Question 1

FL-3.1.3 (K2) Explain the difference between static and dynamic techniques, considering objectives, types of defects to be identified, and the role of these techniques within the software lifecycle

Justification

a) Not correct – This is false. Both static and dynamic testing have the same objective to assess the **quality** of the work product. (Syllabus 3.1.3)
b) Not correct – This is false. Both static and dynamic testing have the same objective to find defects as soon as possible. (Syllabus 3.1.3)
c) Not correct – This is false. Defects found using static testing are easier to find and fix. (Syllabus 3.1.3)
d) **Correct** – This is true. Static testing can be used to improve the consistency and internal quality of work products, while dynamic testing typically focuses on externally visible behaviors. (Syllabus 3.1.3)

Question 2

FL-3.1.2 (K2) Use examples to describe the value of static testing

Justification

a) **Correct** – This is true. Static testing prevents defects in design or coding by uncovering omissions, inaccuracies, inconsistencies, ambiguities, and redundancies in requirements. (Syllabus 3.1.2)
b) Not correct – This is not completely true. Static testing decreases both the development and testing cost. (Syllabus 3.1.2)
c) **Correct** – This is true. Static testing increases development productivity (e.g., due to improved design, more maintainable code). (Syllabus 3.1.2)
d) Not correct – This is false. Run time issues can be found only by dynamic testing. (Syllabus 3.1.3).

Question 3

FL-3.2.3 (K2) Explain the differences between different review types: informal review, walkthrough, technical review and inspection

Justification

a) Not Correct- As it is a safety-critical system it requires a more formal review process. Inspection is best suited for this.
b) Not Correct- Informal review is not suited for review of design documents for a safety-critical system.
c) **Correct-** Inspection is best suited for review of design documents for a safety-critical system. (Syllabus 3.2.3)
d) Not Correct- Walkthrough is not suited for review of design documents for a safety-critical system.

Question 4

FL-3.2.2 (K1) Recognize the different roles and responsibilities in a formal review

Justification

a) Not correct- It is not the responsibility of Facilitator.
b) Not correct- It is not the responsibility of Reviewers.
c) Not correct- It is not the responsibility of the Author.
d) **Correct** – It is the responsibility of the **Management**. (Syllabus 3.2.2)

Question 5

FL-3.2.1 (K2) Summarize the activities of the work product review process

Justification

a) Not correct- These activities are not part of the planning phase.
b) **Correct** - These activities are part of the Initiate review phase. (Syllabus 3.2.1)
c) Not correct- These activities are not part of Individual review phase
d) Not correct – These activities are not part of Issue communication and analysis.

Question 6

FL-3.2.4 (K3) Apply a review technique to a work product to find defects

Justification

a) Not correct – This is role-based review and not a perspective-based review.
b) Not correct – This is an ad hoc review, not a perspective-based review.
c) **Correct** – In perspective-based review, reviewer attempts to use the work product under review to generate the product they would derive from it. In this situation, as the end-user/customer representatives are responsible for the acceptance testing, they will try to create a draft of acceptance test cases from the use-cases to see if all the necessary information is included. (Syllabus 3.2.4)
d) Not correct – This is checklist-based review and not a perspective-based review.

4 Test Techniques

Learning Objectives for Test Techniques 116
4.1 Categories of Test Techniques 117
    4.1.1 Categories of Test Techniques and Their Characteristics 118
4.2 Black-box Test techniques 121
    4.2.1 Equivalence partitioning 121
    4.2.2 Boundary Value Analysis 127
    4.2.3 Decision table testing 132
    4.2.4 State transition testing 138
    4.2.5 Use case testing 143
4.3 White box techniques 146
    4.3.1 Statement testing and coverage 148
    4.3.2 Decision testing and coverage 149
    4.3.3 The value of Statement and Decision Testing 150
4.4 Experience-based techniques 151
    4.4.1 Error Guessing 151
    4.4.2 Exploratory testing 153
    4.4.3 Checklist-based testing 154
4.5 Relevant glossary terms and keywords 156
4.6 Quiz 158
4.7 Answers 164

Learning Objectives for Test Techniques

Following learning objectives are covered in this chapter:

4.1 Categories of Test Techniques

FL-4.1.1   (K2) Explain the characteristics, commonalities, and differences between black-box test techniques, white-box test techniques, and experience-based test techniques

4.2 Black-box Test Techniques

FL-4.2.1   (K3) Apply equivalence partitioning to derive test cases from given requirements

FL-4.2.2   (K3) Apply boundary value analysis to derive test cases from given requirements

FL-4.2.3   (K3) Apply decision table testing to derive test cases from given requirements

FL-4.2.4   (K3) Apply state transition testing to derive test cases from given requirements

FL-4.2.5   (K2) Explain how to derive test cases from a use case

4.3 White-box Test Techniques

FL-4.3.1   (K2) Explain statement coverage

FL-4.3.2   (K2) Explain decision coverage

FL-4.3.3   (K2) Explain the value of statement and decision coverage

4.4 Experience-based Test Techniques

FL-4.4.1   (K2) Explain error guessing

FL-4.4.2   (K2) Explain exploratory testing

FL-4.4.3   (K2) Explain checklist-based testing

4.1 Categories of Test Techniques

The purpose of a test technique is to identify test conditions, test cases and test data.

The choice of which test techniques to use depends on a number of factors. Some of these include:

- **Complexity of system**- e.g. simple or complex system
- **External requirements** - regulatory standards, customer or contractual requirements
- **Perception of risk** - level and type of risk (e.g. high-security risk software used in the banking industry)
- **Development lifecycle**- e.g. Waterfall, Agile
- **Documentation details** – Detailed specification or high-level specification available
- **Testers knowledge**- the experience of the tester in a particular test technique
- **Cost and Schedule**- project budget and project timelines
- **Defects**- the type of defects expected
- **Tools**- available tool in the organization, some test techniques require certain tools to be available.

Some techniques are more applicable to certain situations and test levels; others are applicable to all test levels. Testers generally use a combination of test techniques while writing the test cases to achieve the best results from the test effort.

The test techniques used to derive test cases can range from very informal (little to no documentation) to very formal (detailed documentation).

The level of documentation depends on the following

- Context of testing
- Maturity of test and development processes
- Time constraints
- Safety or regulatory requirements
- Knowledge and skills of the people involved
- Software development lifecycle model

4.1.1 Categories of Test Techniques and Their Characteristics

It is a classic distinction to denote test techniques as black-box, white-box or experience-based.

Black-box test techniques (also called behavioral or behavior-based techniques) are used to derive and select test conditions or test cases, based on the analysis of the test basis documentation.

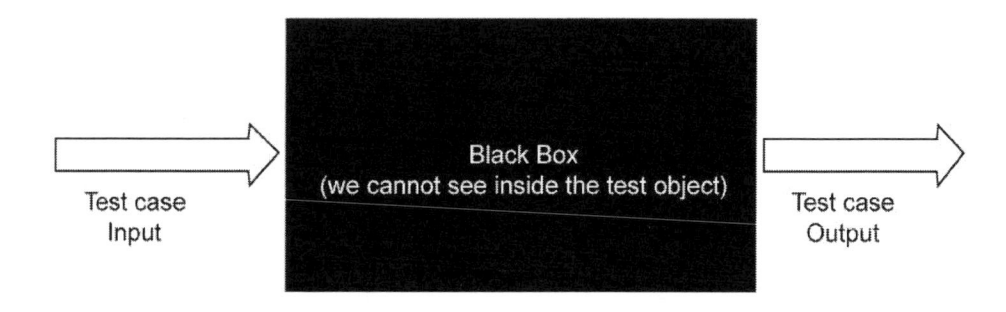

Black-box testing

These techniques concentrate on the inputs and outputs of the test object without reference to its internal structure. They can be used for both functional and non-functional testing.

Common features of black-box test techniques:

- Test conditions, test cases, and test data are derived from a test basis that may include software requirements, specifications, use cases, and user stories
- Test cases may be used to detect gaps between the requirements and the implementation of the requirements, as well as deviations from the requirements
- Coverage is measured based on the items tested in the test basis and the technique applied to the test basis

White-box test techniques (also called structural or structure-based techniques) are based on an analysis of the architecture, detailed design, internal structure, or the code of the test object.

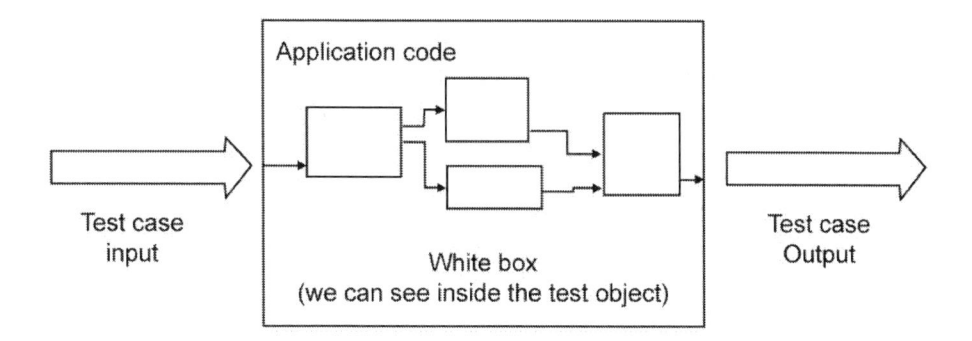

White-box testing

These techniques focus on the structure of the test object.

Common features of white-box test techniques:

- Test conditions, test cases, and test data are derived from a test basis that may include code, software architecture, detailed design, or any other source of information regarding the structure of the software
- Coverage is measured based on the items tested within a selected structure (e.g., the code or interfaces) and the technique applied to the test basis

Experience-based test techniques leverage the experience of developers, testers, and users to design, implement, and execute tests

Experience-based testing

Black-box and white-box testing may also be combined with experience-based techniques to leverage the experience of developers, testers, and users to determine what should be tested.

Common features of experience-based test techniques:

- The knowledge and experience of people (e.g. testers, developers, users and other stakeholders) are used to derive the test cases. This includes:
    - Knowledge of the usage of the software
    - Knowledge of the environment of software
    - Knowledge about likely defects and their distribution.

Experienced-based techniques would commonly be used to augment more structured test techniques. They are often used when there is insufficient supporting test basis or none. For example, a tester based on his experience might use a surname of 'Roger-water' or 'O'Neal' to test whether these special characters are permitted within the name field in the system.

The international standard (ISO/IEC/IEEE 29119-4) contains descriptions of test techniques and their corresponding coverage measures.

4.2 Black-box Test techniques

In black-box testing, the program is viewed as a 'black box', in the sense that the box is opaque and its internal activity is therefore not visible to the tester. The tester feeds in input data and observes output data, without any details of the internal system. Test cases are designed to reflect the specified behavior of the component or system under test.

The following black box techniques are covered in the foundation syllabus:
- Equivalence Partitioning
- Boundary Value Analysis
- State Transition Testing
- Decision Table Testing
- Use Case Testing.

All of these techniques are dynamic test techniques resulting in test cases which are run after executing the code.

4.2.1 Equivalence partitioning

Most of the systems contain a large number of possible inputs and outputs. Testing the system considering all of them is nearly impossible. In such cases, the technique of equivalence partitioning may be helpful as it assists the tester in defining the reduced number of test cases that can effectively test the system.

Partitioning is used to create equivalence classes (often called equivalence partitions) which are sets of values that are processed in the same manner. By selecting **one representative value from a partition**, coverage for all the items in the same partition is assumed.

Equivalence partitions (or classes) can be found for both valid data and invalid values.

- Valid values are accepted by the system. An equivalence partition containing valid values is called a "**valid equivalence partition**."
- Invalid values are values that should be rejected by the system. An equivalence partition containing invalid values is called an "**invalid equivalence partition**."
- Partitions can be identified for any data element related to the test object, including **inputs, outputs, internal values, time-related values** (e.g., before or after an event) and for **interface parameters** (e.g., integrated components being tested during integration testing).
- Each value must belong to one and only one equivalence partition.

- Any partition may be divided into sub partitions if required
- When **invalid equivalence partitions** are used in test cases, they should be tested **individually** and not combined with other invalid equivalence partitions. This will ensure that failures are not masked as several failures may occur at the same time but only one is visible, causing the other failures to be undetected.

Example:

A bank allow the customers to apply for an online bank account. The customer age is taken as input and if customer age is between 18 to 60 years they can proceed with the online application. The customer age field only accepts integer values greater than zero.

If we use the equivalence partitioning technique to test this system, we can divide the input (customer age) into three equivalence classes or partitions as shown below.

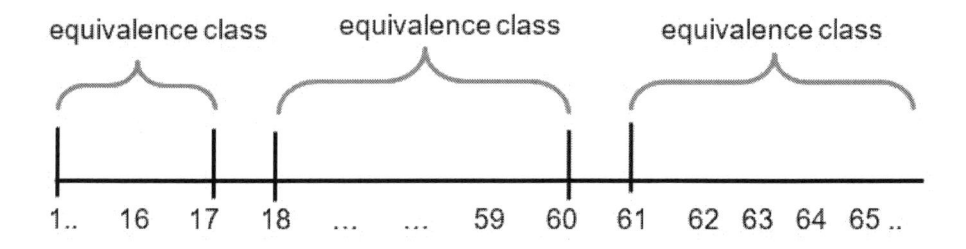

```
equivalence class       equivalence class        equivalence class

1..   16   17   18   ...   ...   59   60   61   62  63  64  65 ..
```

We can take any one of the values from each equivalence class. e.g. 15, 20, 65. Thus, three test cases will be sufficient.

In this case, the values from the first and third partitions are invalid values and values from the second partitions are valid values.

If there is slight variation in the question and the system accepts any integers then the partitions will increase. There will be one partition to test negative values (age entered with '-' sign) and one partition to test age entered as zero.

So, to verify all the equivalence classes we will need five test cases. They will check the system with (-15), (0), (15), (20), (65) (one value from each partition)

Coverage

Coverage is measured as the number of partitions tested by at least one value divided by the number of partitions that have been identified. It is normally expressed in percentage.

For our online bank account example if we test the system only with value 15 then the coverage will be 1/3*100 =33.33%.

Using multiple values for a single partition does not increase the coverage percentage.

To achieve 100% coverage with this technique, test cases must cover all identified partitions (including invalid partitions) by using a minimum of one value from each partition. If we test the above system with value 15, 20, 65 then the coverage will be 100% as all the partitions are covered.

Exam takeout

Equivalence Partitioning is a test design technique that divides the inputs and outputs of a system into **different classes or partitions**. Selecting **one value** from each partition will ensure the coverage for all the values from that partition.

> **Exercise:**
>
> Consider using equivalence partitioning technique to test a system that accepts the name of the months as inputs and display the following output message based on the following rules
>
> - For a 30-day month (e.g. June) the message is "Standard month"
> - For a 31-day month (e.g. January) the message is "Extended month"
> - For the 28/29-day month (February) the message is "Small month"

Solution:

To solve this problem first identify both input and output classes as defined within the specification

Input
- All month with "30" days – Apr, Jun, Sep, Nov
- All month with "31" days – Jan, Mar, May, Jul, Aug, Oct, Dec
- All month with "28/29" days – Feb

Output
- "Standard month"
- "Extended month"
- "Small month"

Identify at least one value from each class to be a representative value

Test Number	Input Partition	Input Data	Expected Result
1	All month with "30" days	Jun	"Standard month"
2	All month with "31" days	Mar	"Extended month"
3	All month with "28/29" days	Feb	"Small month"

Using the Equivalence Partitioning method for the input partition a test is defined that will test each class. Therefore, the above three tests are sufficient as they are ensuring that all the input and output classes are covered.

It is important to ensure that all the output conditions are represented too by the tests.

Exercise:

The system calculates annual family energy rebate based on the following set of rules:

- $850 on annual income up to $40,000
- $550 on annual income over $40,000 and up to $100,000
- $150 on annual income over $100,000 and up to $200,000
- No rebate on annual income over $200,000

Derive a set of equivalence partitions to test this system.

Solution:

To solve this problem first identify both input and output classes as defined in the question

Input

1. equivalence partition: $0 < Annual income ≤ $40,000
2. equivalence partition: $40,000 < Annual income ≤ $100,000
3. equivalence partition: $100,000 < Annual income ≤ $200,000
4. equivalence partition: $200,000 < Annual income.

Output

There are two output partitions- No rebate or rebate

There are four distinct classes or partitions for input. One value from each partition is sufficient to test the system.

e.g. ($25,000), ($95,000), ($150,000), ($250,000)

These input values will also test all the output partitions.

Exercise:

A council system calculates the monthly waste levy based on the type of residence.

- For the house, the levy is $10
- For the apartment, the levy is $9
- For townhome, the levy is $9
- For vacant land, the levy is $1

Retirement living are exempted from any levy. Find out the minimum number of test cases by applying equivalence partitioning test technique?

When the values are discrete, each enumeration value is an equivalence class itself. Therefore, the input and output partitions are:

Input

1. House
2. Apartment
3. Townhouse
4. Villa
5. Retirement livings

Output

1. $0
2. $1
3. $9
4. $10

We need minimum one test to test each input partition by applying Equivalence Partitioning test technique. Each test case for these input partitions will also cover all the output partitions ($0, $1, $9, $10)

Therefore, five tests are sufficient to test all the valid partitions.

4.2.2 Boundary Value Analysis

Boundary value analysis (BVA) is an extension of equivalence partitioning, but can only be used when the partition is ordered, consisting of numeric or sequential data. **The first and last value of a partition are its boundary values**.

Behavior at the boundaries of equivalence partitions is more likely to be incorrect than behavior within the partitions. In most of the cases, both specified and implemented boundaries may be displaced to positions above or below their intended positions, may be omitted altogether, or may be supplemented with unwanted additional boundaries. Boundary value analysis and testing will reveal almost all such defects by forcing the software to show behaviors from a partition other than the one to which the boundary value should belong.

There are two ways to approach BVA: **two value** or **three value** testing. With **two value testing**, the **boundary value** (on the boundary) and the value that is just **over the boundary** (by the smallest possible increment) are used. For **three value** boundary testing, the values **before**, **on** and **over the boundary** are used. The values are based on the risk associated with the item being tested, with the three-boundary approach being used for the higher risk items.

For both Equivalence Partitioning and Boundary Value Analysis, the output values of the set classes also need an examination to ensure that they are valid.

Example:

A bank allow the customers to apply for an online bank account. The customer age is taken as input and if customer age is between 18 to 60 years they can proceed with the online application. The customer age field only accepts integer values greater than zero.

If we use boundary value analysis to test this system, we need to first divide the input (customer age) into three equivalence classes or partitions as shown below.

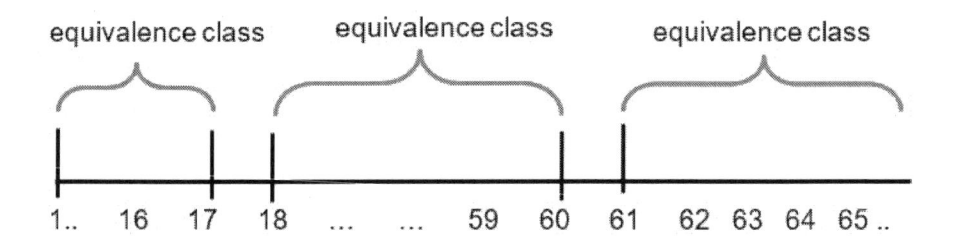

```
equivalence class    equivalence class    equivalence class
      ⌒                    ⌒                    ⌒
  |   |   |   |                    |   |   |   |   |   |   |
  1.. 16  17  18  ...        ...  59  60  61  62  63  64  65 ..
```

For the second equivalence class, the first and last value of the partitions are the boundary values

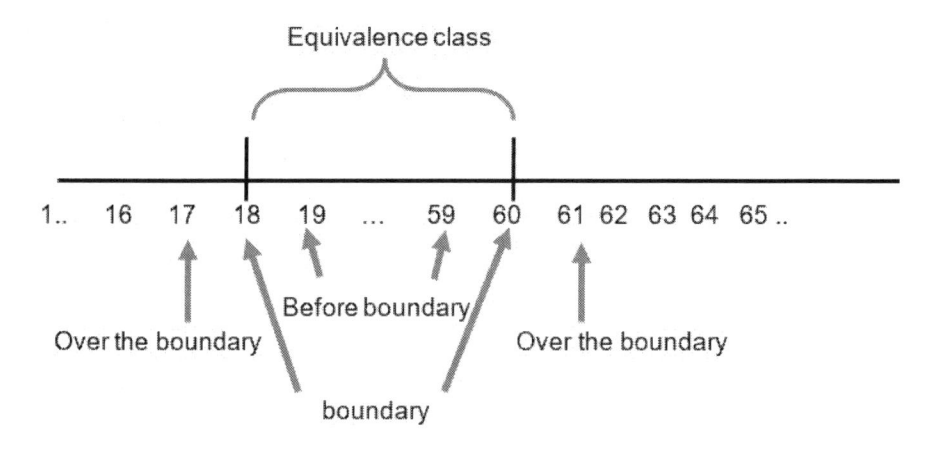

```
                    Equivalence class
                          ⌒
          |   |   |   |         |   |   |   |   |   |   |
      1.. 16  17  18  19  ...  59  60  61  62  63  64  65 ..
              ↑   ↑   ↑         ↑   ↑   ↑
                     Before boundary
          ↑                              ↑
   Over the boundary              Over the boundary
                         boundary
```

The two-point boundary value requires that 2 values are tested at each boundary; **one on the boundary** and **one 'just' over the boundary**. (i.e. 17, 18 and 60, 61)

The three-point boundary value requires that 3 values are tested at each boundary; **one 'just' before the boundary, one on the boundary** and **one 'just' over the boundary**. (i.e. 19, 18, 17 and 59, 60, 61)

Boundary value analysis can be applied at all test levels. It is relatively easy to apply and its defect finding capability is high. Boundary value and equivalence partitioning are usually used together to design test cases.

Coverage

Coverage is determined by taking the number of boundary conditions that are tested dividing by the number of identified boundary conditions (either using the two value or three value method). This is normally expressed as a percentage.

Exam takeout

Boundary Value Analysis (BVA) checks the **minimum** and **maximum** value (or **first** and **last** values) of a partition as its boundary values. It can be applied to both valid and invalid boundaries. The technique is considered an extension of Equivalence partitioning

---

Exercise:

The system calculates annual family energy rebates based on the following set of rules:

- $850 on annual income up to $40,000
- $550 on annual income over $40,000 and up to $100,000
- $150 on annual income over $100,000 and up to $200,000
- No rebate on annual income over $200,000

Find out the set of values (in years) identified by two-point boundary value analysis?

The following partitions can be identified:

1. Annual income ≤ $40,000 Two-point boundaries
   40,000, 40,001

2. $40,001 ≤ Annual income ≤ $100,000 Two-point boundaries
   40,000, 40,001, 100,000, 100,001

3. $100,001 ≤ Annual income ≤ $200,000 Two-point boundaries
   100,000, 100,001, 200,000, 200,001

4. $200,000 < Annual income. Two-point boundaries
   200,000, 200,001

Therefore, after removing the duplicates the values for two-point boundary value analysis will be (40,000), (40,001), (100,000), (100,001), (200,000), (200,001)

> **Exercise:**
>
> An online train reservation system calculates ticket concession based on the passenger's age. The age can only be entered as a positive number, without any decimal or fractional parts.
>
> For passenger aged 5 or less the concession is 100%.
> For passenger aged over 5 and up to 18, the concession is 60%.
> For passenger aged over 18 and up to 60, there is no concession.
> For a passenger aged more than 60, the concession is 50%.
>
> Find out the set of values identified by two-point boundary value analysis?

The following partitions can be identified:

1.	– 5	Two-point boundaries 5, 6
2.	6 – 18	Two-point boundaries 5, 6, 18, 19
3.	19 – 60	Two-point boundaries 18, 19, 60, 61
4.	61 –	Two-point boundaries 60, 61

The values for two-point boundary value analysis will **5, 6, 18, 19, 60, 61**

Exercise:

The bank offers variable interest rates based on the balance in the saving account

- For amount $500 or less the rate is 0.25%
- For amount over $500 and up to $1000, the rate is 0.5%
- For any amount more than $1000 the rate is 1%

Find out all set of values ($) for three-point boundary value analysis?

The following input partitions can be identified:

1.   – 500   Three-point boundaries 499.99, 500, 500.01
2.   500.01 – 1000   Three-point boundaries 500, 500.01, 500.02, 999.99, 1000, 1000.01
3.   1000.01 –   Three-point boundaries 1000, 1000.01, 1000.02

The values for three-point boundary value analysis will be (499.99), (500), (500.01), (500.02), (999.99), (1000), (1000.01), (1000.02).

These input values will test all the output partitions (0.25%, 0.5% and 1%) also.

4.2.3 Decision table testing

Decision tables are used to test the interaction between combinations of conditions. They can be used to record complex business rules that a system must implement. This technique may be applied to all situations when the action of the software depends on several logical decisions.

A decision table is made up of two parts, **the conditions (or inputs)** and **Actions (or outputs)**.

Creating decision tables:

- Testers identify **conditions** (often inputs) and the **resulting actions** (often outputs) of the system.
- The conditions as placed at the **top** of the table and the actions at the **bottom**.
- Each column corresponds to a decision rule that defines a unique combination of conditions which results in the execution of the actions associated with that rule.
- The values of the conditions and actions are usually shown as Boolean values (true or false) or discrete values (e.g. red, yellow, green) or ranges of numbers.

For conditions:

- Y means the condition is true (may also be shown as T or 1)
- N means the condition is false (may also be shown as F or 0)
- '—' or N/A means the value of the condition does not matter

For actions:

- Y means the action should occur (may also be shown as X or T or 1)
- Blank means the action should not occur (may also be shown as – or N or F or 0)

Example:

A new online system is developed for the travel insurance company. User can select followings options based on their status:
- Disabled
- Ex-defence personal
- Pensioner

If user has selected any one of the above options, they are eligible for 25% discount.

The number of rules for the decision table can be derived from the number of conditions. The number of rules for the decision table is equal to $2^{(no\_of\ conditions)}$. In this example, there are 3 conditions, therefore, $2^3 = 8$ rules are required to consider all the inputs.

The decision table for this system will look like below:

Rules →	1	2	3	4	5	6	7	8
Conditions ↓								
Disabled	Y	N	Y	N	Y	N	Y	N
Ex-defence personal	N	N	Y	Y	N	N	Y	Y
Pensioner	N	N	N	N	Y	Y	Y	Y
Actions								
Discount	Y	N	Y	Y	Y	Y	Y	Y

A full decision table has enough columns (test cases) to cover every combination of conditions. By deleting columns that do not affect the outcome, the number of test cases can decrease considerably. For example by removing impossible combinations of conditions

Coverage

The common minimum coverage standard for decision table testing is to have at least one test case per decision rule in the table. This typically involves covering all combinations of conditions. Coverage is measured as the number of decision rules tested by at least one test case, divided by the total number of decision rules, normally expressed as a percentage.

Note: In the Foundation level examination you are asked to interpret a decision table. You are not asked to calculate the number of permutations or to draw a decision table.

Exam takeout
Decision table provides a clear method to verify testing of all pertinent combinations of conditions and to verify that all possible combinations are handled by the software under test.
The goal of decision table testing is to ensure that every combination of conditions, relationships and constraints are tested.

Exercise:

A new system is developed to accept the visa application online. To use the system applicants must first enter the passport details. The system will check the validity of the passport and only then the applicant is prompted to enter nationality and credit card details.

Following decision table has been designed to test the logic and decide whether the application can be accepted.

	R1	R2	R3	R4	R5	R6	R7	R8
Conditions								
Valid Passport	N	N	N	N	Y	Y	Y	Y
Eligible country	Y	Y	N	N/A	Y	Y	N	N
Valid credit card	Y	N	Y	N/A	Y	N	Y	N
Actions								
Application Accepted	N	N	N	N	Y	N	N	N

1. What will be the application outcome for Denis who is having the nationality of a country eligible for a visa and a valid passport but his credit card has expired?

2. Which of the test cases wouldn't occur in a real situation and can be eliminated from the decision table?

---

1. Denis falls under **R6** hence his application won't be accepted.

2. As mentioned in the question, the user is prompted to provide nationality and credit card details **only if the passport is valid**. So, all the test cases where the applicant is able to enter nationality and credit card detail when the passport is invalid (**R1, R2, R3**) can be eliminated.

Exercise:

Following decision table is used to select the Lab Test based on the existing health conditions of the patients.

Conditions	Rule 1	Rule 2	Rule 3	Rule 4	Rule 5	Rule 6	Rule 7	Rule 8
Diabetic	N	N	N	N	Y	Y	Y	Y
High blood pressure	N	N	Y	Y	N	N	Y	Y
Asthma	N	Y	N	Y	N	Y	N	Y
Actions								
Lab Test A	Y	Y	N	N	Y	Y	N	N
Lab Test B	Y	Y	Y	Y	N	N	N	N
Lab Test C	Y	N	Y	Y	Y	N	Y	Y

- Which Lab Tests are suitable for the patient who is diabetic but not sure about other conditions?
- Which Lab Tests are suitable for the patient who is having only Asthma?

- Lab Test A and C as **Rule 5, Rule 6, Rule 7 and Rule 8** are applicable.
- Lab Test A and B as **Rule 2** is applicable.

Exercise:

Consider a system for a train ticket pricing with the following set of rules.

- For traveller under age 6, there is no fare.
- For traveller aged 6-23, if they have a student concession card, they are charged concession fare otherwise they are charged an Adult off-peak fare.
- If they are over 23 and travelling during off-peak time then the adult off-peak fare is applied, otherwise, they will be charged peak prices.
- If an adult over 23 has an Annual discovery pass, they are given a 10% discount on all fares.

The following decision table has been designed to test the logic and decide whether the user qualifies for the discount.

Rules / Conditions	Rule 1	Rule 2	Rule 3	Rule 4	Rule 5	Rule 6	Rule 7
Age	1-5	6-23	6-23	Over 23	Over 23	Over 23	Over 23
Student concession card	N/A	Y	N	N/A	N/A	N/A	N/A
Travel time	N/A	N/A	N/A	Off-peak	Peak	Off-peak	Peak
Annual Discovery pass	N/A	N/A	N/A	N	N	Y	Y
Actions							
Free travel	Y	N	N	N	N	N	N
Concession fare	N	Y	N	N	N	N	N
Adult off-peak fare	N	N	Y	Y	N	Y	N
Adult peak fare	N	N	N	N	Y	N	Y
25% discount	N	N	N	N	N	Y	Y

Find out which fares are applicable for following travellers

- Richard who is 23-years-old and has an Annual discovery pass, he is travelling during off-peak hours.
- Sarah who is 30-years-old is travelling during peak hours with her 2-year-old son.

Richard fall under **Rule 3** hence Adult off-peak fare is applicable for him.

Sarah fall under **Rule 5 and her son falls under Rule 1** hence Adult off-peak fare and free travel are applicable for them respectively.

4.2.4 State transition testing

Some components or systems transition from one state to another state and perform certain actions based on the events. The response to these events is dependent on current conditions or previous events or history that have occurred since the component or system was initialized. The previous events or history can be summarized using the concept of states.

State transition testing is concerned with the inputs and resulting actions when a system changes its mode of operation. Each mode of operation is referred to as its state, and the action of changing state is called a transition.

State transition testing is used to test the ability of the software to enter into and exit from defined states via valid and invalid transitions. **Events** cause the software to **transition from state to state** and to perform **actions**. Events may be qualified by conditions which influence the transition path to be taken. For example, a login event with a valid username/password combination will result in a different transition than a login event with an invalid password.

A state transition table shows all valid transitions and potentially invalid transitions between states, as well as the events, conditions, and resulting actions for valid transitions. **State transition diagrams** normally show only the valid transitions and exclude the invalid transitions.

Tests can be designed to cover a typical sequence of states, to exercise all states, to exercise every transition, to exercise specific sequences of transitions, or to test invalid transitions.

Consider a simple example of a TV having an ON and OFF button. Its starting state is OFF and the end state is Play. In order to change state, the ON button is pressed, this is the input. The resulting action of this input is that the TV starts playing. If the OFF button is pressed when the TV is playing it will result in the end state of TV off.

A state transition diagram would look like this:

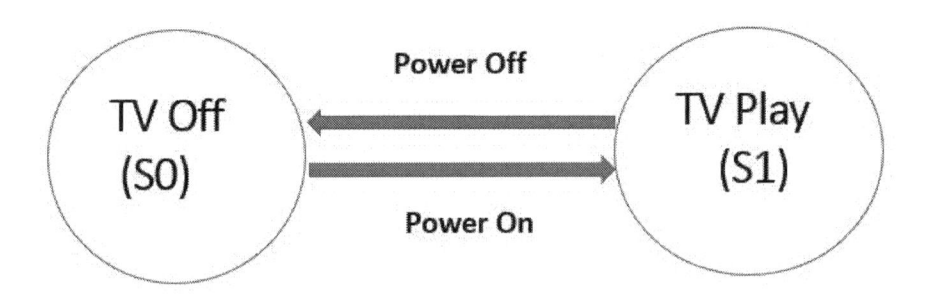

```
            Power Off
 ┌──────┐ ◄──────────── ┌──────┐
 │TV Off│                │TV Play│
 │ (S0) │ ────────────► │ (S1) │
 └──────┘    Power On    └──────┘
```

The following can be summarised from the above state transition diagram

- **States-** TV OFF(S0) and TV Play(S1)
- **Transitions between states** - (S0→ S1, S1→ S0)
- **Inputs (events) that trigger state changes (transitions)** – Power on, Power off
- **Actions which may result from those transitions** - TV will play or it will be off

A state transition table can be created for the above state transition diagram. All the states are on the left-hand side of the table, and all the triggers(events) are across the top.

Now to derive the value of each cell of the table input the trigger at the top of the current state. When the current state is **S0** and '**Power on**' trigger is applied the resulting state (end-state) is **S1**. When the current state is **S1** and '**Power Off**' trigger is applied the resulting state (end-state) is **S0**. These are valid transactions because when the trigger is applied the end state is different from the current state.

When the current state is **S1** and '**Power on**' trigger is applied nothing happens. Similarly, when the current state is **S0** and '**Power off**' trigger is applied nothing happens. These are invalid transactions or "null" transactions (denoted by '-').

	Power on	**Power off**
S0	S1	-
S1	-	S0

Looking at the table, there are 2 valid transactions and 2 invalid or "null" transactions (denoted by '-'). Therefore, a total of **4 tests** are required to fully test the system. (2 positive test cases and 2 negative test cases)

State transition testing is applicable for any software that has defined states and has events that will cause the transitions between those states (e.g., changing screens). State transition testing can be used at any level of testing. Embedded software, web applications, control systems (traffic light controllers) and any other type of transactional systems are good candidates for this type of testing.

Coverage

Coverage is commonly measured as the number of identified states or transitions tested, divided by the total number of identified states or transitions in the test object, normally expressed as a percentage

The minimum acceptable degree of coverage is to have visited every state and traversed every transition. 100% transition coverage will guarantee that every state is visited and every transition is traversed unless the system design or the state transition model (diagram or table) is defective.

Exam takeout
State transition diagrams show only the valid transitions and exclude the invalid transitions, whereas the **state transition table** shows all the valid and invalid transitions.

Exercise:

Consider the following state transition diagram showing the different states and input requests for a TV.

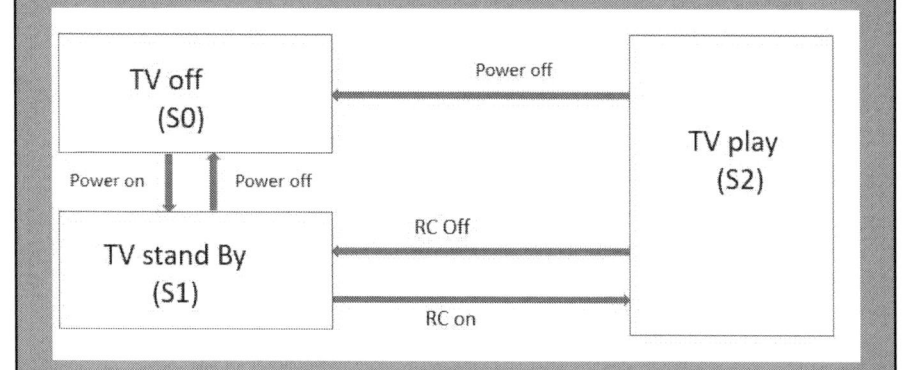

```
                          Power off
    TV off    ←─────────────────────────
    (S0)                                  
                                          TV play
   Power on  │ ↑ Power off                (S2)
            ↓ │                           
                          RC Off
   TV stand By  ←─────────────────────
   (S1)                                  
                          RC on
```

Find out the number of test cases required to test all the valid and invalid transactions?

A state transaction table can be created for the above state transition diagram. All the states are on the left-hand side of the table, and all the triggers(events) are across the top.

Now to derive the value of each cell of the table input the trigger at the top of the current state.

Example: When the current state is **S0** and '**Power on**' trigger is applied the resulting state (end-state) is **S1**. This is a valid transaction because when the trigger is applied the end state is different from the current state.

When the current state is **S1** and '**Power on**' trigger is applied nothing happens. Therefore, this is an invalid transaction or "null" transaction (denoted by '-').

	Power on	Power off	RC Off	RC On
S0	S1	-	-	-
S1	-	S0	-	S2
S2	-	S0	S1	-

From the table, there are 5 valid transactions and 7 invalid or "null" transactions (denoted by '-').

Therefore, a total of **12 tests are** required to fully test the system.

(test cases for valid transactions = 5, test cases for invalid transactions = 7)

Exercise:

The state transition diagram for a system is shown below:

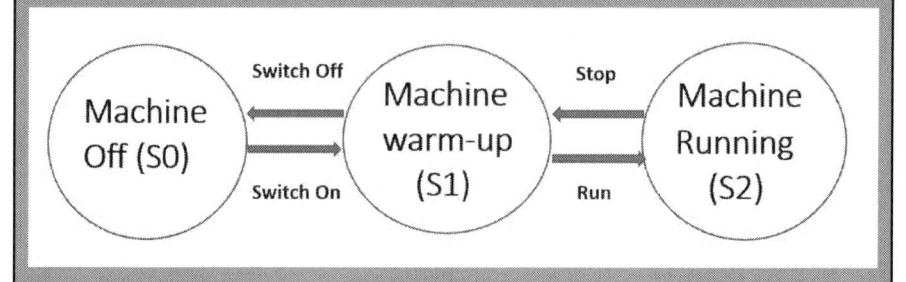

```
                  Switch Off                    Stop
    ┌─────────┐ ←──────────  ┌─────────┐ ←──────────  ┌─────────┐
    │ Machine │              │ Machine │              │ Machine │
    │ Off (S0)│              │ warm-up │              │ Running │
    │         │ ──────────→  │  (S1)   │ ──────────→  │  (S2)   │
    └─────────┘  Switch On   └─────────┘     Run      └─────────┘
```

Find out all the invalid test cases required to test the system?

A state transaction table can be created for the above state transition diagram. All the states are on the left-hand side of the table, and all the triggers(events) are across the top.

Now to derive the value of each cell of the table input the trigger at the top of the current state.

Example: When the current state is **S0** and '**Switch on**' trigger is applied the resulting state (end-state) is **S1**. This is a valid transaction because when the trigger is applied the end state is different from the current state.

When the current state is **S1** and '**Switch on**' trigger is applied nothing happens. Therefore, this is an invalid transaction or "null" transaction (denoted by '-').

	Switch on	Switch off	Run	Stop
S0	S1	-	-	-
S1	-	S0	S2	-
S2	-	-	-	S1

From the table, there are 4 valid transactions and 8 invalid or "null" transactions (denoted by '-'). Invalid tests are below:

Test case	1	2	3	4	5	6	7	8
Start state	S0	S1	S1	S2	S2	S2	S0	S0
Input	Switch off	Switch on	Stop	Switch on	Switch off	Run	Run	Stop
Expected final state	S0	S1	S1	S2	S2	S2	S0	S0

4.2.5 Use case testing

A system's functionality can be defined by a set of use-cases. The purpose of the use-case is to describe the interactions with the system from the user's perspective. Use cases are associated with the external party called an **actor** which may refer to human users, external hardware, or other system interacting with the **subject** which may be the current system or component to which the use case is applied.

Each use case specifies some behavior that a subject can perform in collaboration with one or more actors. A use case can be described by interactions and activities, as well as preconditions, postconditions, and any alternative flows. Interactions between the actors and the subject may result in changes to the state of the subject. Interactions may be represented graphically by workflows, activity diagrams, or business process models.

A use case can include possible variations of its basic behavior, including exceptional behavior and error handling (system response and recovery from programming, application and communication errors, e.g., resulting in an error message). Tests are designed to exercise the defined behaviors (basic, exceptional or alternative, and error handling).

Use-Cases are built around the interactions of the actor with the system. By focusing on each actor in isolation, with actions which provide value to the system, the risk of building an unsatisfactory system can be minimized.

Specifications are written using use-cases which often incorporate use-case diagrams, showing the interaction of subject and the actors.

An example of a use case diagram of a system which has functions to print, scan, fax, and copy is shown below:

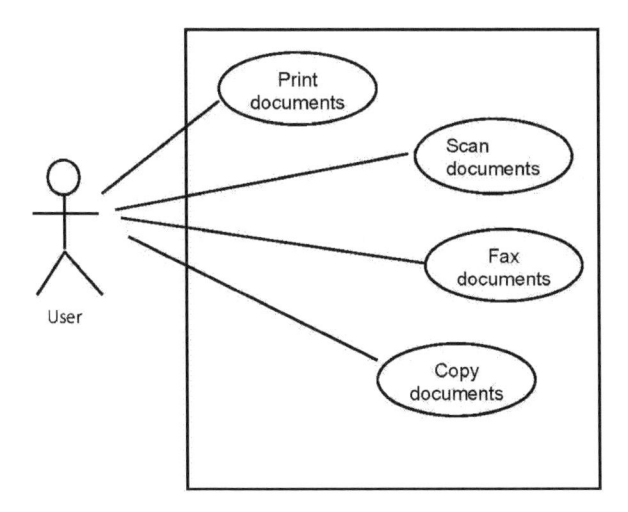

A use case diagram for a multi-function printer

The system being described is a multi-function printer. The multi-function printer has a user that interacts with the system. The user is the '**Actor**' and multi-function printer is the '**Subject**'. In this example, there are four ways in which the user can interact with the Multi-function printer. These ways of interacting or using the system are called 'use cases' and they are depicted using an eclipse shape with a brief description of the function that the user is using:

- Print documents
- Scan documents
- Fax documents
- Copy documents

The arrow between the actor and the use case shows a relationship between the user and the functions that they may utilize. These use case diagrams are designed to be easy to understand high-level diagrams showing the functions of a system and the actors that use them.

In order to get more detail, the tester would need to refer to an associated document called the 'Use Case Description'. The Use case description describes the flow of events between the actor and the system in order to execute a use-case. This description should be in natural language, using simple and consistent wording, incorporating a common glossary of terms.

Considering the use-case 'Print documents' as an example, the use case description might be something like:

Use Case ID	MFP001
Description	Print document
Actors	User
Pre-conditions	Multi-function printer is switched on. User device is connected to the Multi-function printer.
Post-condition	Document is printed.
Trigger/event	User clicks on the 'Print' option from their device
Main Scenario (Basic path)	
1. The user selects the 'Print' option from the document 2. The user selects the Multi-function printer as a printer from the printer list. 3. The user clicks on the print button.	
Extensions (alternative path)	
3a. The user cancels the "Print job" before printing starts	
Exceptional path	
1. Printing of document will stop when Printer is showing error message "Paper jam" 2. Printing of document will stop when Printer is showing error message "Load paper to tray" 3. Printing of documents will stop when Printer is showing error message "Toner is low"	

From this flow of events, the tester would create the test case(s). The flow of events become the steps within the test case(s) and the tester has to identify the input parameters and the corresponding expected results.

The use-case terminates with a 'success means' or post-condition – the observable result – which in this case is the 'happy scenario' that the document is printed. However, there are alternative flows to some of the steps which will also need to be tested. Use-case testing primarily focuses on the system from a user perspective.

Coverage

Coverage can be measured by the number of use case behaviors tested divided by the total number of use case behaviors, normally expressed as a percentage.

Exam takeout
In use case testing, test cases are written based on the use cases which describes user interactions with the system.

4.3 White-box techniques

White-box testing is based on an internal structure of the test object.

White-box tests look 'inside the box' at the code that makes up the system's individual functions. White-box techniques help in designing test cases based on the internal structure and design of the component or system under test. The component code is analyzed and broken down into executable areas. Each area is then exercised by constructing test cases that force the program to traverse specific paths. The aim is to ensure that all required structural elements can be exercised without mishap. Functional behavior is not the focus of attention, although the expected outcome of a structural test can and should be predicted and verified.

Foundation level syllabus covers two white-box techniques:

- Statement testing
- Decision testing

These techniques are most commonly used at the component test level.

Consider the following code:

1. READ X
2. Y=500
3. IF X < Y THEN
4. PRINT 'X
5. ELSE
6. PRINT 'Y'
7. END IF

Flowchart for the code:

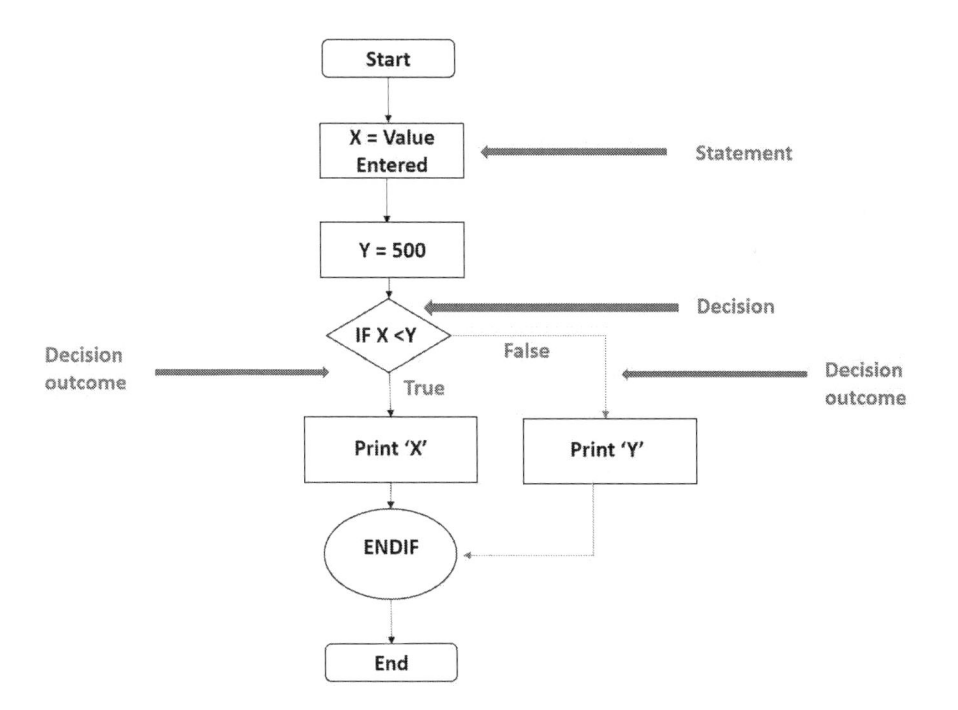

Exam takeout
Both statement and Decision Testing are most commonly used at the component test level.

4.3.1 Statement testing and coverage

Statement testing is a technique designed to test every potential executable statement in a program. An executable statement is a statement which, when compiled, is translated into object code, and which will be executed procedurally when the program is running and may perform an action on data.

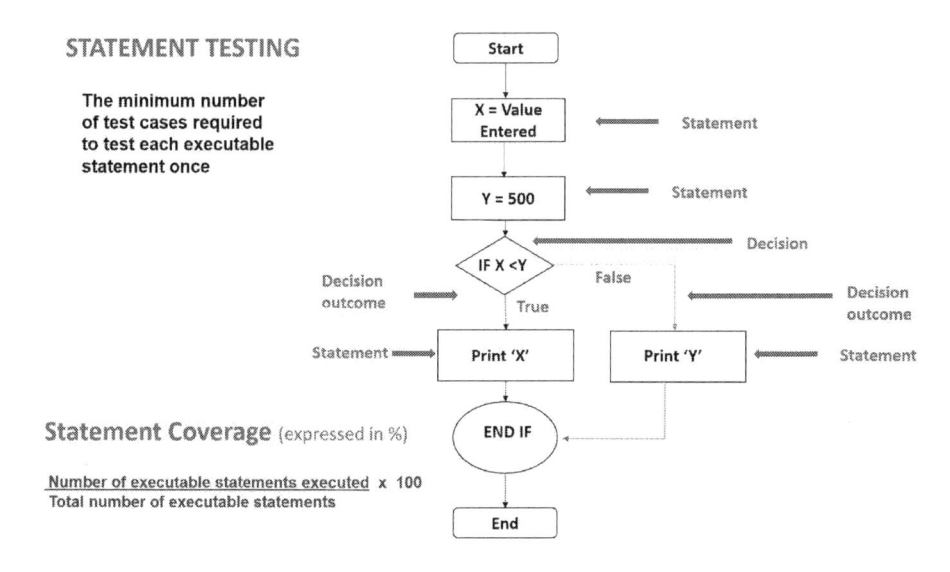

STATEMENT TESTING

The minimum number of test cases required to test each executable statement once

Statement Coverage (expressed in %)

$$\frac{\text{Number of executable statements executed}}{\text{Total number of executable statements}} \times 100$$

Statement testing and coverage

Statement coverage is measured as the number of statements executed by the tests divided by the total number of executable statements in the test object, normally expressed as a percentage.

Exam takeout
Statement testing exercises all the potential executable statements in the code.

4.3.2 Decision testing and coverage

Decision testing focuses on decision points in a program. It looks at each outcome of the decision. Decision testing exercises the decisions in the code and tests the code that is executed based on the decision outcomes. To do this, the test cases follow the control flows that occur from a decision point (e.g., for an IF statement, one for the true outcome and one for the false outcome; for a CASE statement, test cases would be required for all the possible outcomes, including the default outcome).

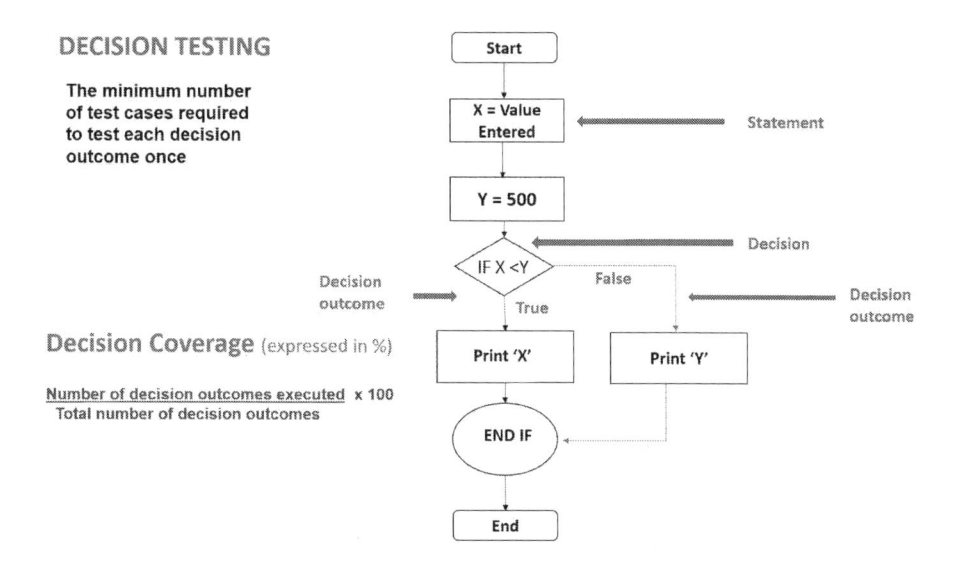

DECISION TESTING
The minimum number of test cases required to test each decision outcome once

Decision Coverage (expressed in %)

$$\frac{\text{Number of decision outcomes executed}}{\text{Total number of decision outcomes}} \times 100$$

Decision testing and coverage

Decision coverage is measured as the number of decision outcomes executed by the tests divided by the total number of decision outcomes in the test object, normally expressed as a percentage.

Exam takeout
Decision testing exercises the decisions in the code and tests the code that is executed based on the decision outcomes.

4.3.3 The value of Statement and Decision Testing

- When **100% statement coverage** is achieved, it ensures that all executable statements in the code have been tested at least once, but it does not ensure that all decision logic has been tested.
- Statement coverage helps to find defects in code that were not exercised by other tests.
- Statement testing may provide less coverage than decision testing.
- When **100% decision coverage** is achieved, it executes all decision outcomes, which includes testing the true outcome and also the false outcome, even when there is no explicit false statement (e.g., in the case of an IF statement without an else in the code).
- Decision coverage helps to find defects in code where other tests have not taken both true and false outcomes.
- Achieving 100% decision coverage guarantees 100% statement coverage but 100% statement coverage does not guarantees 100% decision coverage.

Exam takeout
Achieving 100% decision coverage guarantees 100% statement coverage (but not vice versa).

4.4 Experience-based techniques

As the name suggests, these techniques make use of the experiences of the tester. In this technique test cases are derived based on:

- **Testers skill-** Which specific areas are more prone to defects?
- **Testers intuition-** Where can failures appear?
- **Testers experience with similar applications-** Where did failures occur in prior versions of the application or in similar applications?
- **Testers experience with similar technologies-** What are the known problems when using similar technology?

These techniques are applied when the software has been delivered and as such are dynamic test techniques. These techniques can be helpful in identifying tests that were not easily identified by other more systematic techniques.

Experience-based testing may be a good alternative to more structured approaches where system documentation is poor, testing time is severely restricted or the test team has strong expertise in the system to be tested. However, these techniques may be inappropriate where systems requiring detailed test documentation, high-levels of repeatability or ability to precisely assess test coverage. The coverage and effectiveness of these techniques may widely vary depending on the tester's approach and experience. This is the reason they mostly are used to complement the other structured approaches.

Coverage

Coverage is very difficult to assess and, in most cases, not measurable when using these techniques.

The most widely practiced techniques for Experience-based testing are:

- Error guessing
- Exploratory testing
- Checklist-based Testing

4.4.1 Error Guessing

Error guessing is a technique used to anticipate the occurrence of errors, defects, and failures, based on the tester's knowledge, including:

- Application behavior in the past
- Typical kind of errors tend to be made
- Failures from similar applications

In this technique testers first create a list of possible errors, defects, and failure based on their experience, defect and failure data, or from common knowledge about why software fails.

For example, based on their experience if the testers expect the software will fail when an invalid password is entered, tests will be designed to enter a variety of different values in the password field to verify if the similar error was indeed made and has resulted in a defect that can be seen as a failure when the tests are run. Another scenario would be to make a list of common defects which are found while entering following data into input fields:

- Null values
- Blanks
- Spaces
- Long names being truncated
- Names containing apostrophes being rejected as invalid

Knowing that all these defects can actually become failures the tester determines the best methods to designs test cases that can be specifically used to uncover the resulting defects.

Error guessing can be useful to identify special tests not easily captured by formal techniques, especially when applied after more formal approaches.

However, this technique may yield widely varying degrees of effectiveness, depending on the tester experience.

Error guessing is done primarily during integration and system testing but can be used at any level of testing. This technique is often used with other techniques and helps to broaden the scope of the existing test cases. Error guessing can also be used effectively when testing a new release of the software to test for common errors before starting more rigorous and scripted testing. Checklists and taxonomies may be helpful in guiding the testing.

This technique is often used with other techniques and helps to broaden the scope of the existing test cases. Error guessing can also be used effectively when testing a new release of the software to test for common mistakes and errors before starting more rigorous and scripted testing.

Coverage

Coverage is difficult to assess and varies widely with the capability and experience of the tester. It is best used by an experienced tester who is familiar with the types of defects that are commonly introduced in the type of code being tested. Error guessing is commonly used, but is frequently not documented and so may be less reproducible than other forms of testing

> **Exam takeout**
>
> Error guessing technique is most suitable when a detailed list of possible defects and failures is available.
>
> For error guessing to be truly beneficial, defect and failure lists should be derived from the combined experience and skills of all the test team members.

4.4.2 Exploratory testing

In exploratory testing, test cases are not pre-defined but design, execution, test logging, and learning are carried out dynamically during test execution.

In exploratory testing tester dynamically adjusts test goals during execution and prepares only lightweight documentation. The test results help in learning more about the system, and to create tests for the areas that may require more testing.

Exploratory testing is characterized by the tester simultaneously learning about the system and its defects, planning the testing work to be done, designing and executing the tests, and reporting the results.

To make exploratory testing more effective a **session-based testing** is used to structure the activity. In session-based testing, exploratory testing is conducted within a defined time-box, and the tester uses a test charter containing test objectives to guide the testing. The tester may use test session sheets to document the steps followed and the discoveries made.

Exploratory testing is mostly used in the situations where the **specifications are not available** or are **not adequate** for other testing techniques or there is **significant time pressure** for testing. Exploratory testing is often used to augment other more formal testing and to serve as a basis for the development of additional test cases.

Exploratory testing is commonly used in the project where reactive test strategies are used.

> **Exam takeout**
>
> In Exploratory testing, test cases are not predefined but created and executed during test execution. This technique is most suitable when there are few or inadequate specifications and/or there is significant time pressure on testing.
>
> **Session-based testing-** Exploratory testing performed in defined time-box.
>
> **Test Charter-** Documentation of the goal or objective for a test session in exploratory testing.
>
> **Test session sheet-** Used for documenting the steps followed and findings.

4.4.3 Checklist-based testing

In checklist-based testing, testers use a checklist to design, implement, and execute the test case. These checklists are high-level, generalized list of items to be noted, checked, or remembered, or a set of rules or criteria against which a product has to be verified. The tester may also use an existing checklist or modify or create a new checklist during the analysis. These checklists are built based on standards, experience, knowledge about what is important for the user, or an understanding of why and how software fails.

Example: For testing a GUI based application the tester may use a standard user interface checklist.

Checklist-based testing is used most effectively in projects with an experienced test team that is familiar with the software under test or familiar with the area covered by the checklist (e.g., to successfully apply a user interface checklist, the tester needs to be familiar with user interface testing or the specific software under test).

As checklists are high-level and tend to lack the detailed steps commonly found in test cases and test procedures, the knowledge of the tester is used to fill in the gaps. Apart from the lack of detailed steps, checklists are low maintenance and can be applied to multiple similar releases.

Checklists can be created to support various test types, including functional and non-functional testing and can be used for any level of testing. Checklists are also used for regression testing and smoke testing. In the absence of detailed test cases, checklist-based testing can also provide guidelines and a degree of consistency.

Coverage

The coverage is as good as the checklist but, because of the high-level nature of the checklist, the results will vary based on the tester who executes the checklist.

Exam takeout

Checklists are created using standards, tester experiences and knowledge.

The checklists serve as a manual outlined of what needs to be checked.

These checklists can be used at any test level but are common for smoke and regression testing.

Summary

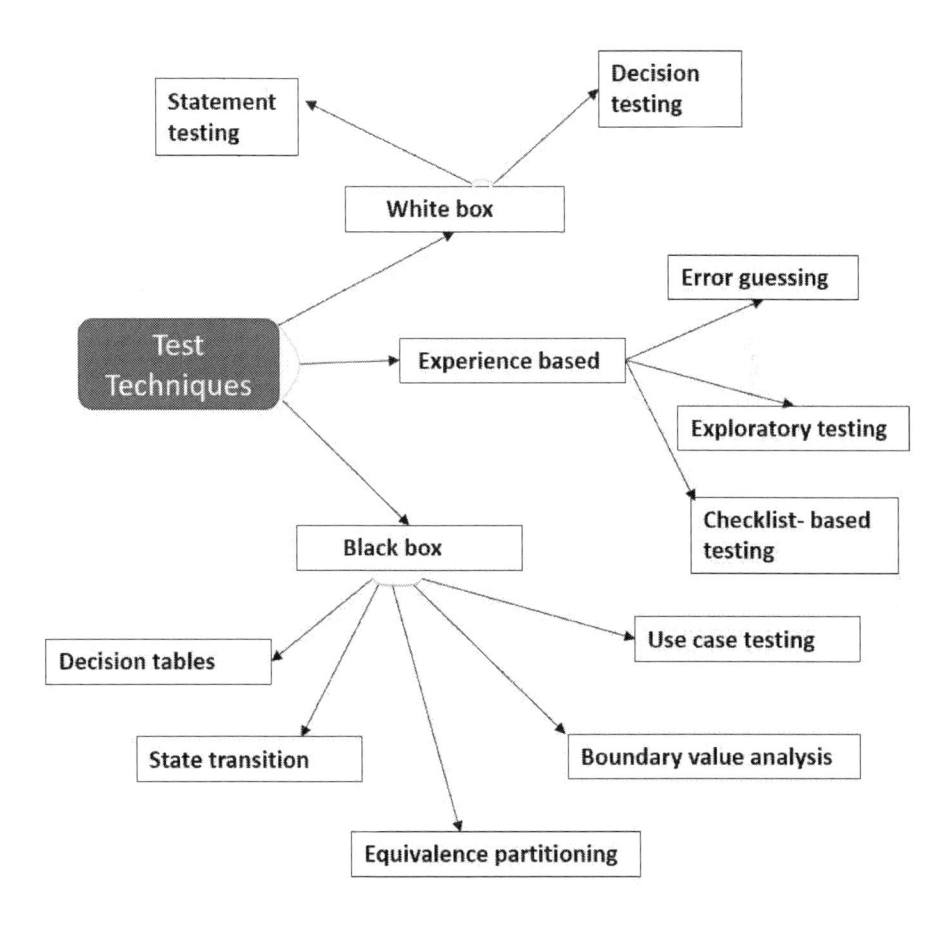

```
                                    Decision
            Statement               testing
            testing
                          White box
                                              Error guessing
            Test
        Techniques ──────► Experience based
                                              Exploratory testing

                                              Checklist-based
                          Black box           testing

                                              Use case testing
    Decision tables

        State transition              Boundary value analysis

                      Equivalence partitioning
```

4.5 Relevant glossary terms and keywords

Glossary term	Definition
Black box testing	Testing, either functional or non-functional, without reference to the internal structure of the component or system.
Black-box test technique	A test technique based on an analysis of the specification of a component or system.
Boundary value	A minimum or maximum value of an ordered equivalence partition.
Boundary value analysis	A black-box test technique in which test cases are designed based on boundary values.
Boundary value coverage	The coverage of boundary values.
Coverage	The degree to which specified coverage items have been determined or have been exercised by a test suite expressed as a percentage.
Code coverage	The coverage of code.
Checklist-based testing	An experience-based test technique whereby the experienced tester uses a high-level list of items to be noted, checked, or remembered, or a set of rules or criteria against which a product has to be verified.
Decision	A type of statement in which a choice between two or more possible outcomes controls which set of actions will result.
Decision coverage	The coverage of decision outcomes.
Decision table testing	A black-box test technique in which test cases are designed to exercise the combinations of conditions and the resulting actions shown in a decision table.
Decision table	A table used to show sets of conditions and the actions resulting from them.
Equivalence partition	A subset of the value domain of a variable within a component or system in which all values are expected to be treated the same based on the specification.
Equivalence partitioning	A black-box test technique in which test cases are designed to exercise equivalence partitions by using one representative member of each partition.
Error guessing	A test technique in which tests are derived on the basis of the tester's knowledge of past failures, or general knowledge of failure modes.

Glossary term	Definition
Experienced based testing	Testing based on the tester's experience, knowledge and intuition.
Experience-based test technique	A test technique only based on the tester's experience, knowledge and intuition.
Exploratory testing	An approach to testing whereby the testers dynamically design and execute tests based on their knowledge, exploration of the test item and the results of previous tests.
Statement	An entity in a programming language, which is typically the smallest indivisible unit of execution.
Statement testing	A white-box test technique in which test cases are designed to execute statements.
Statement coverage	The coverage of executable statements.
State transition testing	A black-box test technique in which test cases are designed to exercise elements of a state transition model.
State transition	A transition between two states of a component or system.
Test basis	The body of knowledge used as the basis for test analysis and design.
Test case	A set of preconditions, inputs, actions (where applicable), expected results and postconditions, developed based on test conditions. [ISO 29119]
Test case specification	Documentation of a set of one or more test cases. [ISO 29119]
Test technique	A procedure used to define test conditions, design test cases, and specify test data.
Test script	A sequence of instructions for the execution of a test.
Traceability	The degree to which a relationship can be established between two or more work products
White-box test technique	A test technique only based on the internal structure of a component or system.
White box testing	Testing based on an analysis of the internal structure of the component or system.
Use case testing	A black-box test technique in which test cases are designed to exercise use case behaviors.

4.6 Quiz

Question 1

Which one of the following TWO statements correctly describes the white-box test technique?

a) It is a technique where test cases are derived based on the analysis of the architecture.
b) It is a technique where test cases are derived based on the knowledge of the developers.
c) It is a technique where test cases are derived based on the expected use of the software.
d) It is a technique where test cases are derived based on the technical design of the system.

Question 2

How is decision coverage measured?

a) It is measured as the number of decision outcomes executed by the tests divided by the total number of decision outcomes in the code, expressed as a percentage.
b) It is measured as the number of decision outcomes of the source code executed by test cases that are passed, expressed as a percentage.
c) It is measured as the number of decision outcomes divided by total number of executable statements expressed as a percentage.
d) It is measured as all the false decision outcomes in the source code divided by the total number of decision outcomes in the code expressed as a percentage

Question 3

Consider the system built to automatically calculate the government childcare rebates based on the total income of the family. There is a maximum rebate of 80% for combined income less than $40,000. There is no rebate if the combined income is more than or equal to $120,000.

Rest of the rules for calculating the rebate are:

- 70% for total income from $40,000 and less than $50,000
- 60% for total income from $50,000 and less than $60,000
- 50% for total income from $60,000 and less than $70,000
- 25% for total income from $70,000 and less than $90,000
- 10% for total income from $90,000 and less than $120,000

What is the minimum number of test cases required to cover all valid equivalence partitions for calculating the childcare rebate?

a) 5
b) 8
c) 6
d) 7

Question 4

Consider the following statement:

"The section of code contains multiple executable statements but no decision logic (there are no IF, loops or case statements)"

Which of the following is correct with respect to the above scenario?

a) For this scenario, one test is sufficient to achieve 100% statement coverage
b) For this scenario, more than two tests are required to achieve 100% statement coverage
c) For this scenario, two tests are sufficient to achieve 100% statement coverage
d) For this scenario, additional information is required to get the exact number of tests to achieve 100% statement coverage.

Question 5

An airline baggage system allows bags weighing 10kg or less to be carried as hand luggage for free. Bags weighing above 10kg but less or equal to 20kg must be checked-in and incur no charge. Bags weighing more than 20kg are checked-in and incur a charge.

Bags are weighed in units of 1kg and cannot weigh 0 kg.

How many tests will be required to test all set of values for the three-point boundary value analysis technique?

a) 10
b) 9
c) 8
d) 7

Question 6

For testing a GUI based application, exploratory testing will be the MOST suitable test technique for which scenario?

a) The user interactions with GUI based application are captured in business process diagrams.
b) The requirements specifications for GUI based application are incomplete.
c) A detailed list of possible defects for GUI based applications is available.
d) A standard user interface checklist for GUI based application is available.

Question 7

The Department of Motor Vehicles uses the following decision table to calculate the punishment for the drivers who are not following the safety-rules.

Conditions	Rule 1	Rule 2	Rule 3	Rule 4	Rule 5
Seat belt offence	N	N	Y	Y	N/A
Alcohol/drug offence	N	N	N	N	Y
Speeding offence	N	Y	N	Y	N/A
Actions					
Demerit points	N	Y	N	Y	Y
Penalty	N	N	Y	Y	Y
Licence suspension	N	N	N	N	Y

What would be the punishment for following drivers?

- Harry was caught for speeding and alcohol/drug offence.
- Jack who caught only for seat belt offence.

    a) Harry – Demerit points and Penalty;
       Jack – Demerit points.
    b) Harry – Demerit points, Penalty & Licence suspension;
       Jack – Demerit points & Penalty.
    c) Harry – Demerit points, Penalty & Licence suspension;
       Jack – Penalty.
    d) Harry – Licence suspension;
       Jack – Demerit points.

Question 8

Consider a system for an electronic device which can display either time or the date based on the user selection.

Following state transition diagram shows the different states and input requests for this device.

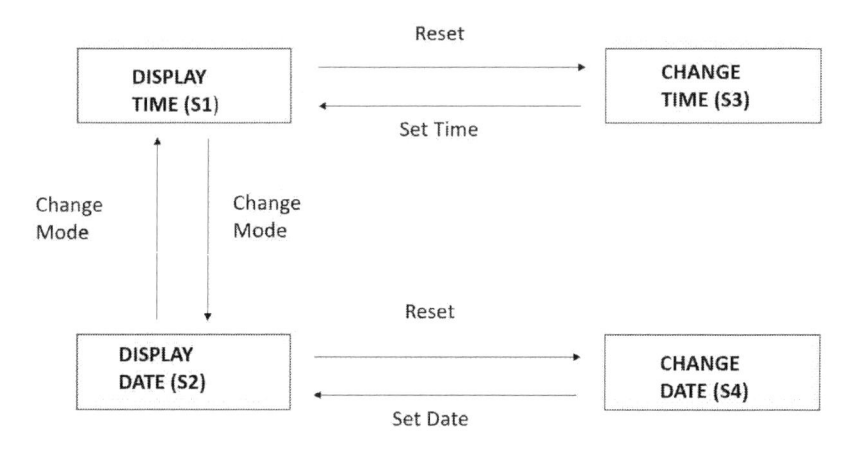

How many tests are required to test all the valid transactions for the above state transition diagram?

a) 16 tests.
b) 6 tests.
c) 9 tests.
d) 10 tests.

Question 9

Which of the following TWO statements correctly describe use case testing?

a) Use cases testing can cover the interaction of external hardware with other component or systems.
b) Use cases testing covers the interactions between the actors and the system that accomplish some goal.
c) Use case testing is only applicable for system and acceptance test level.
d) Use case testing focus on basic behavior and does not cover the error handling.

Question 10

The system for income tax department calculates the tax based on the individual income earned during the financial year. Income up to $20,000 is exempted from tax, thereafter tax is calculated based on the following rules:

- For income up to $45,000 the tax is $5672 plus 4% of the amount above $20,000

- For income more than $45,000 and up to $75,000 the tax is $6670 plus 6% of the amount above $45,000

- For income more than $75,000 and up to $120,000 the tax is $9628 plus 8% of the amount above $75,000

- For income more than $120,000 the tax is $19,672 plus 10% of the amount above $120,000

Which of the following groups of numbers cover all the valid equivalence classes?

a) ($20,000), ($45,000), ($75,000), ($120,000)
b) ($20,000), ($45,000), ($75,000), ($120,000), ($150,000)
c) ($0), ($20,000), ($45,000), ($75,000), ($120,000)
d) ($45,000), ($75,000), ($120,000), ($150,000)

4.7 Answers

1	2	3	4	5	6	7	8	9	10
A, D	A	D	A	C	B	C	B	A,B	B

Question 1

FL-4.1.1 (K2) Explain the characteristics, commonalities, and differences between black-box test techniques, white-box test techniques and experience-based test techniques

Justification

a) **Correct** – This is a white-box test technique.
b) Not correct – This is experience-based test technique.
c) Not correct – This is experience-based test technique.
d) **Correct** – This is a white-box test technique.

Question 2

FL-4.3.2 (K2) Explain decision coverage

Justification

a) **Correct** – Decision testing exercises all the decisions in the code. Decision coverage is measured as the number of decision outcomes executed by the tests divided by the total number of decision outcomes in the code. It is normally expressed as a percentage. (Syllabus 4.3.2)
b) Not correct – Decision coverage is not measured based on test execution results.
c) Not correct – Decision coverage is not measured based on executable statements.
d) Not correct – It is not only the false decision but both true and false decisions which are required to get the coverage.

Question 3

FL-4.2.1 (K3) Apply equivalence partitioning to derive test cases from given requirements

Justification

a) Not correct – see explanation in d).
b) Not correct – see explanation in d).
c) Not correct – see explanation in d).
d) **Correct** – Partitions are as below:

1. equivalence partition: 0 < Rebate < $40,000
2. equivalence partition: $40,000 < Rebate < $50,000
3. equivalence partition: $50,000 < Rebate < $60,000
4. equivalence partition: $60,000 < Rebate < $70,000
5. equivalence partition: $70,000 < Rebate < $90,000
6. equivalence partition: $90,000 < Rebate < $120,000
7. equivalence partition: $120,000 < Rebate.

Therefore, a minimum of **seven** tests will be required to test all the valid partitions.

Question 4

FL-4.3.1 (K2) Explain statement coverage

Justification

a) **Correct** – If there are no decisions is the code then one test should be sufficient to achieve 100% statement coverage.
b) Not correct – Check explanation for a)
c) Not correct – Check explanation for a).
d) Not correct – There is enough information provided, check explanation for a).

Question 5

FL-4.2.2 (K3) Apply boundary value analysis to derive test cases from given requirements

Justification

The following partitions can be identified:

1. – 10   Three-point boundaries 9,10,11
2. 11 – 20   Three-point boundaries 10, 11, 12, 19, 20,21
3. 21 –   Three-point boundaries 20,21,22

Test are required for boundaries 9, 10, 11, 12, 19, 20, 21, 22

Therefore, total tests required to test three-point boundaries are 8.
Thus:

a) Not correct – see the justification above.
b) Not correct – see the justification above.
c) **Correct** – see the justification above.
d) Not correct – see the justification above.

Question 6

FL-4.4.2 (K2) Explain exploratory testing

Justification

a) Not correct-When business process diagrams are available, **use case testing** is most suitable. (Syllabus 4.2.5)
b) **Correct**-When there are few inadequate specifications, **exploratory testing** is most suitable. (Syllabus 4.4.2)
c) Not correct- When a details list of possible defects and failures is available, **error guessing technique** is most suitable. (Syllabus 4.4.1)
d) Not correct- When a standard user interface checklist is available, **checklist-based testing** is most suitable. (Syllabus 4.4.2)

Question 7

FL-4.2.3 (K3) Apply decision table testing to derive test cases from given requirements

Justification

Harry falls under **Rule 5**, hence demerit points, Penalty & licence suspension.

Jack falls under **Rule 3**, hence only penalty.

Hence,

a) Not correct- see explanation above.
b) Not correct- see explanation above.
c) **Correct** - see explanation above.
d) Not correct - see explanation above.

Question 8

FL-4.2.4 (K3) Apply state transition testing to derive test cases from given requirements

Justification

A state transition table can be created for the state transition diagram in the question. All the states are on the left-hand side of the table, and all the triggers(events) are across the top.

Now to derive the value of each cell of the table input the trigger at the top of the current state.

Example: When the current state is **S1** and **'Change Mode'** trigger is applied the resulting state (end-state) is **S2**. This is a valid transaction because when the trigger is applied the end state is different from the current state.

When the current state is **S1** and **'Set Time'** trigger is applied nothing happens. Therefore, this an invalid transaction or "null" transaction (denoted by '-').

	Change Mode	Reset	Set Time	Set Date
S1	S2	S3	-	-
S2	S1	S4	-	-
S3	-	-	S1	-
S4	-	-	-	S2

From the table, there are 6 valid transactions and 10 invalid or "null" transactions (denoted by '-').

Therefore, test cases for valid transactions =6, Test cases for invalid transactions = 10.

a) Not correct – see the explanation above.
b) **Correct** – see the explanation above.
c) Not correct – see the explanation above.
d) Not correct – see the explanation above.

Question 9

FL-4.2.5 (K2) Explain how to derive test cases from a use case

Justification

a) **Correct** – This describes the use case testing.
b) **Correct** – This describes the use case testing.
c) Not correct – Use case testing is applicable for all test levels.
d) Not correct – Use case testing covers both basic behavior and error handling. (Syllabus 4.2.5)

Question 10

FL-4.2.1 (K3) Apply equivalence partitioning to derive test cases from given requirements

Justification

Valid equivalence partitions are below:

1. $0 < - \leq 20,000$
2. $20,000 < - \leq 45,000$
3. $45,000 < - \leq 75,000$
4. $75,000 < - \leq 120,000$
5. $120,000 < -$

($20,000), ($45,000), ($75,000), ($120,000), ($150,000) covers all the five partitions.

a) Not correct – see explanation above
b) **Correct** – see explanation above.
c) Not correct – see explanation above.
d) Not correct – see explanation above.

5 Test Management

Learning Objectives for Test Management 172
5.1 Test organization 173
    5.1.1 Independent Testing 173
    5.1.2 Tasks of the test manager and tester 175
5.2 Test planning and Estimation 181
    5.2.1 Purpose and content of a Test plan 181
    5.2.2 Test Strategy and Test Approach 183
    5.2.3 Entry criteria and Exit Criteria
          (Definition of Ready and Definition of Done) 186
    5.2.4 Test Execution Schedule 187
    5.2.5 Factors Influencing the Test Effort 189
    5.2.6 Test Estimation Techniques 189
5.3 Test Monitoring and Control 192
    5.3.1 Metrics used in Testing 192
    5.3.2 Purposes, Contents, and Audiences for Test Reports 193
5.4 Configuration management 195
5.5 Risk and testing 197
    5.5.1 Definition of Risk 197
    5.5.2 Product and Project Risks 198
    5.5.3 Risk-based testing and Product Quality 200
5.6 Defects management 203
5.7 Relevant glossary terms and keywords 206
5.8 Quiz 209
5.9 Answers 212

Learning Objectives for Test Management

Following learning objectives are covered in this chapter:

5.1 Test Organization

FL-5.1.1 (K2) Explain the benefits and drawbacks of independent testing

FL-5.1.2 (K1) Identify the tasks of a test manager and tester

5.2 Test Planning and Estimation

FL-5.2.1 (K2) Summarize the purpose and content of a test plan

FL-5.2.2 (K2) Differentiate between various test strategies

FL-5.2.3 (K2) Give examples of potential entry and exit criteria

FL-5.2.4 (K3) Apply knowledge of prioritization, and technical and logical dependencies, to schedule test execution for a given set of test cases

FL-5.2.5 (K1) Identify factors that influence the effort related to testing

FL-5.2.6 (K2) Explain the difference between two estimation techniques: the metrics-based technique and the expert-based technique

5.3 Test Monitoring and Control

FL-5.3.1 (K1) Recall metrics used for testing

FL-5.3.2 (K2) Summarize the purposes, contents, and audiences for test reports

5.4 Configuration Management

FL-5.4.1 (K2) Summarize how configuration management supports testing

5.5 Risks and Testing

FL-5.5.1 (K1) Define risk level by using likelihood and impact

FL-5.5.2 (K2) Distinguish between project and product risks

FL-5.5.3 (K2) Describe, by using examples, how product risk analysis may influence the thoroughness and scope of testing

5.6 Defect Management

FL-5.6.1 (K3) Write a defect report, covering defects found during testing

5.1 Test organization

5.1.1 Independent Testing

Testing can be performed by a person in a specific testing role, or by people in another role (e.g., customers). It is often the case that the creator of a product cannot see its faults. In software development, this can be due to many things. The developer may:

- Be too close to the product to be completely objective
- Be under significant time pressure
- Be more interested in creating new products than reworking existing ones.

A certain degree of independence (avoiding the author bias) is often effective at finding defects and failures. Independence is not, however, a replacement for familiarity and developers can efficiently find many defects in their own code. Independent testing may be carried out at any level of testing

Several **levels of independence** can be defined (from low level of independence to high level):

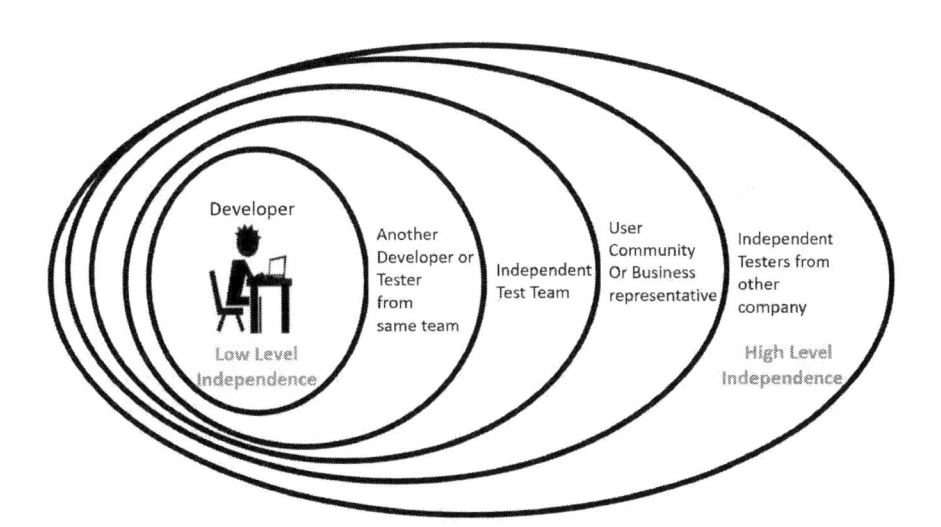

Degree of Independent testing

- Testing is done by the person who wrote the software under test. **(lowest level of independence)**
- Testing is done by another person within the same team as the developer. (other developer or tester testing their colleagues' products)
- Testing is done by an Independent test team or group within the organization, reporting to project management or executive management. This is typically a dedicated testing team. This type of team usually receives the system as a whole for the test. (System testing or Black-box testing)
- Testing is done by the testers from the business community or user community, or with specializations in specific test types such as usability, security, performance, regulatory/compliance, or portability This is generally conducted as a separate stage of testing (e.g. user acceptance testing).
- Testing is done by a tester external to the organization. Testing activities can be carried out working on-site (in-house) or off-site (outsourcing). These testers may have the benefit of being independent of organizational pressures, as well as having the expected knowledge of testing best practice across the industry. **(Highest level of Independence)**

For large, complex or safety-critical projects, it is usually best to have multiple levels of testing, with some or all of the levels done by independent testers.

Key exam take-out

Independent testing is carried out by someone other than the developer **who wrote** the code.

A certain degree of independence often makes the tester more effective at finding defects due to differences between the author's and the tester's cognitive biases.

Potential benefits of test independence include:

- Independent testers are likely to recognize different kinds of failures compared to developers because of their different backgrounds, technical perspectives, and biases
- An independent tester can verify, challenge, or disprove assumptions made by stakeholders during the specification and implementation of the system

- Independent testers from an external organization can report in an upright and objective manner about the system under test without pressure from the organization that hired them

Although the benefits of independent testing usually outweigh the **drawbacks**, it is worthwhile noting some of these drawbacks. They include:

- Isolation from the development team, may lead to a lack of collaboration, delays in providing feedback to the development team, or an adversarial relationship with the development team
- Developers may lose a sense of responsibility for quality
- Independent testers may be seen as a bottleneck
- Independent testers may lack some important information (e.g., about the test object)

5.1.2 Tasks of the test manager and tester

In this syllabus two test roles are covered, test manager and tester. The activities and tasks performed by people in these two roles depend on the project and product context, the people in the roles, and the organization.

The test manager takes the **overall responsibility for the test process** and successful leadership of the test activities. The test management role might be performed by a professional test manager, or by a project manager, a development manager, or a quality assurance manager. In larger projects or organizations, several test teams may report to a test manager, test coach, or test coordinator.

Typical test manager tasks may include:

- Develop or review a test policy and test strategy for the organization
- Plan the test activities by considering the context, and understanding the test objectives and risks. This may include selecting test approaches, estimating test time, effort and cost, acquiring resources, defining test levels and test cycles, and planning defect management
- Write and update the test plan(s)
- Coordinate the test plan(s) with project managers, product owners, and others
- Share testing perspectives with other project activities, such as integration planning

- Initiate the analysis, design, implementation, and execution of tests, monitor test progress and results and check the status of exit criteria (or definition of done) and facilitate test completion activities
- Prepare and deliver test progress reports and test summary reports based on the information gathered
- Adapt planning based on test results and progress (sometimes documented in test progress reports, and/or in test summary reports for other testing already completed on the project) and take any actions necessary for test control
- Support setting up the defect management system and adequate configuration management of testware
- Introduce suitable metrics for measuring test progress and evaluating the quality of the testing and the product
- Support the selection and implementation of tools to support the test process, including recommending the budget for tool selection (and possibly purchase and/or support), allocating time and effort for pilot projects, and providing continuing support in the use of the tool(s)
- Decide about the implementation of the test environment(s)
- Promote and advocate the testers, the test team, and the test profession within the organization
- Develop the skills and careers of testers (e.g., through training plans, performance evaluations, coaching, etc.)

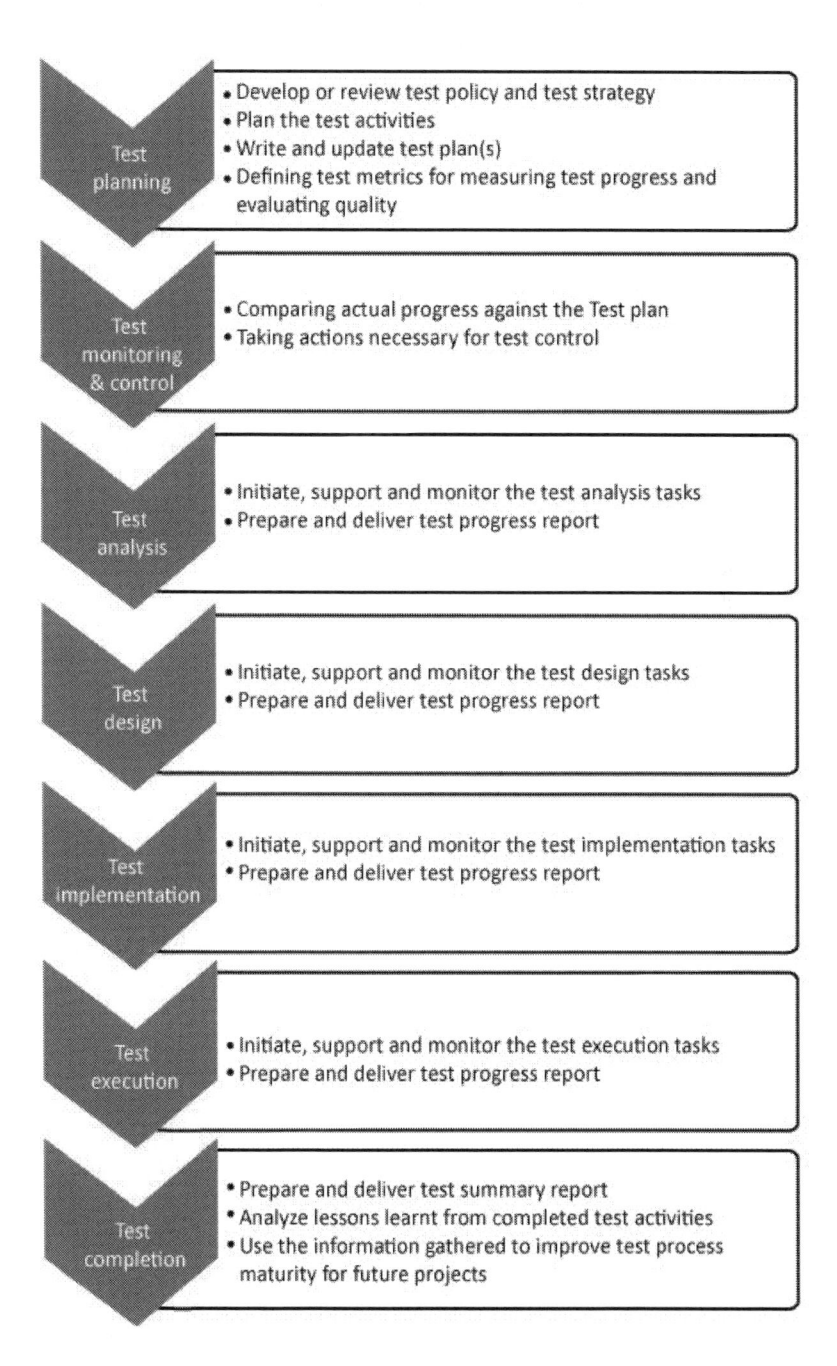

Test planning
- Develop or review test policy and test strategy
- Plan the test activities
- Write and update test plan(s)
- Defining test metrics for measuring test progress and evaluating quality

Test monitoring & control
- Comparing actual progress against the Test plan
- Taking actions necessary for test control

Test analysis
- Initiate, support and monitor the test analysis tasks
- Prepare and deliver test progress report

Test design
- Initiate, support and monitor the test design tasks
- Prepare and deliver test progress report

Test implementation
- Initiate, support and monitor the test implementation tasks
- Prepare and deliver test progress report

Test execution
- Initiate, support and monitor the test execution tasks
- Prepare and deliver test progress report

Test completion
- Prepare and deliver test summary report
- Analyze lessons learnt from completed test activities
- Use the information gathered to improve test process maturity for future projects

Tasks of Test Manager

The way in which the test manager role is carried out varies depending on the software development lifecycle. For example, in Agile development, some of the test manager tasks may be handled by a tester who is working within the Agile team. Some of the tasks that span multiple teams or the entire organization, may be done by test managers, who are also referred as test coaches.

The tester takes the **overall responsibility for the preparation and execution of the test cases for testing.** Typical tester tasks may include:

- Review and contribute to test plans
- Analyze, review, and assess requirements, user stories and acceptance criteria, specifications, and models for testability (i.e., the test basis)
- Identify and document test conditions, and capture traceability between test cases, test conditions, and the test basis
- Design, set up, and verify test environment(s), often coordinating with system administration and network management
- Design and implement test cases and test procedures
- Prepare and acquire test data
- Create the detailed test execution schedule
- Execute tests, evaluate the results, and document deviations from expected results
- Use appropriate tools to facilitate the test process
- Automate tests as needed (may be supported by a developer or a test automation expert)
- Evaluate non-functional characteristics such as performance efficiency, reliability, usability, security, compatibility, and portability
- Review tests developed by others

Test planning
- Review and contribute to test plans.

Test monitoring & control
- Providing actual progress of testing to Test Manager for comparison against the Test plan

Test analysis
- Analyze, review and assess requirements
- Identify and document test conditions
- Capture tracebility between test conditions and test basis

Test design
- Design test cases
- Identify test data & design test environment
- Review test developed by others
- Capture tracebility between test basis, test conditions, test cases

Test implementation
- Develop and prioritize test procedures and create automate test scripts
- Create test suites
- Building test environment and prepare test data
  Verify and update tracebility

Test execution
- Execute tests
- Evaluate the results and documents deviations from expected results

Test completion
- Finalizing and archiving test environment, test data and other testware
- Analyze lessons learnt from completed test activities
- Handover testware to maintenance team

Tasks of Tester

People who work on test analysis, test design, specific test types or test automation may be specialists in these roles.

Depending on the test level and the risks related to the product and the project, different people may take over the role of tester, keeping some degree of independence.

Typically, testers at the component and integration level would-be developers, testers at the acceptance test level would be business experts and users, and testers for operational acceptance testing are likely to be operators.

Exam takeout

Test manager plans, monitors, controls and report the testing activities.

Tester analyze, design, implement and execute the testing activities.

5.2 Test planning and Estimation

Test planning is an important activity in any project. It ensures that there is initial list of tasks and milestones in a baseline plan. This list and milestones can be used to define the shape and size of the test effort and to track progress against. Test planning is important for both new development (greenfield) as well as maintenance (change and fix) projects.

These are some of the common test management documents which are used to manage and plan the testing activities:

- **Test policy**–Which describes the organization's objectives and goals for testing.
- **Test strategy**–Which describes the overall testing approach for the project or program.
- **Test plan** (or project test plan)–Which describes the implementation of the test strategy for a particular project and defines the high level of the test activities being planned. There can be a master test plan of the whole project and multiple level specific test plans for each test level.

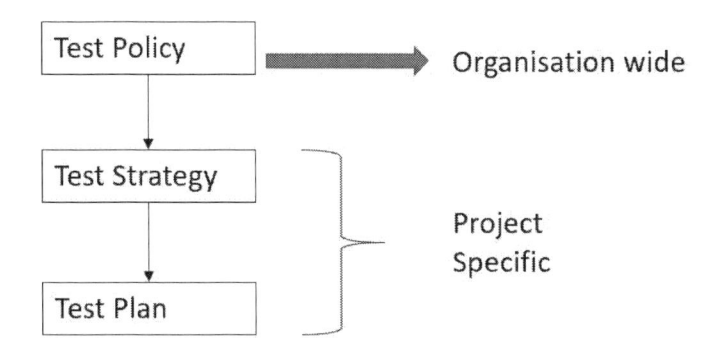

Test Management and Planning Documents

5.2.1 Purpose and content of a Test plan

A test plan outlines the test activity for development and maintenance projects.

Test planning, for the most part, occurs at the initiation of the test effort and involves the identification and planning of all of the activities and resources required to meet the mission and objectives identified in the test strategy.

Planning is influenced by a number of facts such as

- Test policy of the organization
- Test strategy of the organization or project
- Development lifecycles and methods being used
- Scope of testing
- Objectives of testing
- Identified risks
- Project constraints
- Project criticality
- Testability of test object
- Availability of resources

As the project and test planning progress, more information becomes available and more detail can be included in the test plan. Test planning is a continuous activity and is performed throughout the product's lifecycle including the maintenance phase. Feedback from test activities should be used to recognize changing risks so that planning can be adjusted accordingly.

Planning may be documented in a master test plan and in separate test plan for each test level, such as system testing and acceptance testing, or for separate test types, such as usability testing and performance testing.

Test planning activities may include the following and some of these may be documented in a test plan:

- Determining the scope, objectives, and risks of testing
- Defining the overall approach of testing
- Integrating and coordinating the test activities into the software lifecycle activities
- Making decisions about what to test, the people and other resources required to perform the various test activities, and how test activities will be carried out
- Scheduling of test analysis, design, implementation, execution, and evaluation activities, either on particular dates (e.g., in sequential development) or in the context of each iteration (e.g., in iterative development)
- Selecting metrics for test monitoring and control
- Budgeting for the test activities
- Determining the level of detail and structure for test documentation (e.g., by providing templates or example documents)

The content of test plans may vary based on the organization and project. A sample test plan structure and a sample test plan can be found in ISO standard (ISO/IEC/IEEE 29119-3).

Key exam take-out

- **A test plan** is a document outlining test activities for development & maintenance projects.
- Test planning is a continuous activity and is performed throughout the product lifecycle.
- A project may have a Master Test plan and multiple Level Test plans covering each test level.

5.2.2 Test Strategy and Test Approach

A test strategy provides a generalized description of the test process, usually at the product or organizational level. Common types of test strategies include:

- **Analytical,** such as risk-based testing, where tests are designed and prioritized based on the level of risk. This type of test strategy is based on the analysis of some factor (e.g., requirement or risk).

  For example, in requirements-based testing the high-level tests are derived from the requirements, low-level tests are then designed and implemented to cover those requirements. The tests are subsequently executed, often using the priority of the requirement covered by each test to determine the order in which the tests will be run. Test results are also reported in terms of requirements status, e.g., requirement tested and passed, requirement tested and failed, etc.

- **Model-based strategies**, such as operational profiling, where the tests are designed on the basis of some model. This model may be built based on the certain required aspect of the product, such as a function, a business process, an internal structure, or a non-functional characteristic (e.g., reliability) or on actual or anticipated situations of the environment in which the product exists.

  For example, in model-based performance testing of a growing social media site, testers might develop models to show active and inactive users, and resulting processing load, based on current usage and project growth over time. In addition, models might be developed considering the current production environment's hardware, software, data capacity, network, and infrastructure. Models may also be developed for ideal, expected, and minimum throughput rates, response times, and resource allocation.

- **Methodical**, such as quality characteristic-based, where the test team uses a predetermined set of test conditions, such as based on a quality standard (e.g., ISO 25000), a checklist or a collection of generalized, logical test conditions which may relate to a particular domain, application or type of testing (e.g., security testing), or taxonomy of common or likely types of failures, a list of important quality characteristics, or company-wide look-and-feel standards for mobile apps or web pages.

  For example, during maintenance testing of a simple online shopping website, testers might use a checklist that identifies the key functions (new order, modify order, delete orders), attributes, and links for each page. The testers would cover the relevant elements of this checklist each time a modification is made to the site.

- **Process or standard-compliant**, where the test team analyze, design and implement tests based on external rules and standards, such as those following a set of processes defined by a standards committee or other panel of experts, these processes address documentation and use of the test basis etc.

  For example, in projects following Scrum Agile management techniques, in each iteration testers analyze user stories that describe particular features, estimate the test effort for each feature as part of the planning process for the iteration, identify acceptance criteria for each user story, execute tests that cover those conditions, and report the status of each user story (untested, failing, or passing) during test execution.

- **Reactive strategies**, such as defect-based attacks, where testing is not pre-planned but is reactive to the component or system being tested, and the events occurring during test execution. Tests are designed and implemented, and may immediately be executed in response to knowledge gained from prior test results.

  For example, when using exploratory testing on a menu-based application, a set of test charters corresponding to the features, menu selections, and screens might be developed. Each tester is assigned a set of test charters, which they then use to structure their exploratory testing sessions. Testers periodically report the results of the testing sessions to the Test Manager, who may revise the charters based on the findings.

- **Consultative or Directed**, such as user-directed testing, where the test team relies on the advice, guidance, or instructions of stakeholders, business domain experts, or technology experts, who may be outside the test team or outside the organization itself.

For example, in outsourced compatibility testing for a web-based application, a company may give the outsourced testing service provider a prioritized list of different browsers and their versions against which they want to evaluate their application.

- **Regression-averse**, in which the test strategy is motivated by a desire to avoid regression of existing capabilities. This test strategy includes reuse of existing testware (especially test cases and test data), extensive automation of regression tests, and standard test suites.

  For example, when regression testing, a web-based application, testers can use a GUI-based test automation tool to automate the application. Those tests are then executed any time the application is modified.

Different strategies may be combined to come up with an appropriate test strategy. For example, risk-based testing (an analytical strategy) can be combined with exploratory testing (a reactive strategy); they complement each other and may achieve more effective testing when used together.

While the test strategy provides a generalized description of the test process, the test approach tailors the test strategy for a particular project or release. The test approach is the starting point for selecting the test techniques, test levels, and test types, and for defining the entry criteria and exit criteria (or definition of ready and definition of done, respectively).

The tailoring of the strategy is based on decisions made in relation to the following factors in the project such as:

- Project complexity
- Project goals
- Type of product being developed
- Product risk analysis.

The selected approach depends on the context and may consider factors such as

- Risks
- Safety
- Available resources and skills
- Technology
- Nature of the system (e.g., custom-built versus COTS)
- Test objectives
- Regulations

> **Key exam take-out**
> - **Test Strategy** is a document which communicates the **Test Approach** for a given project
> - The Test Approach is subsequently defined and refined in test plans
> - The Test Strategy is guided by the Test Policy
> - The Test Strategy documents the decisions made based on the project's test goals and the risk assessment

5.2.3 Entry Criteria and Exit Criteria (Definition of Ready and Definition of Done)

For each test activity, it is necessary to have a criterion which defines when a given test activity should start and when the activity is complete. This is required for effective control over the quality of the software, and of the testing. The entry and exit criteria should be defined for each test level and test type and will differ based on the test objectives.

Entry Criteria (Definition of Ready in Agile development) define the preconditions for undertaking a given test activity. If entry criteria are not met, it is likely that the activity will prove more difficult, more time-consuming, more costly, and more risky.

Typical entry criteria include:

- Availability of testable requirements, user stories, and/or models (e.g., when following a model-based testing strategy)
- Availability of test items that have met the exit criteria for any prior test levels
- Availability of test environment
- Availability of necessary test tools
- Availability of test data and other necessary resources

Exit Criteria (Definition of Done in Agile development) define what conditions must be achieved in order to declare a test level or a set of tests completed.

Typical exit criteria include:

- Planned tests have been executed
- A defined level of coverage (e.g., of requirements, user stories, acceptance criteria, risks, code) has been achieved

- The number of unresolved defects is within an agreed limit
- The number of estimated remaining defects is sufficiently low
- The evaluated levels of reliability, performance efficiency, usability, security, and other relevant quality characteristics are sufficient

Even without exit criteria being satisfied, it is also common for test activities to be curtailed due to the budget being expended, the scheduled time being completed, and/or pressure to bring the product to market. If the project stakeholders and business owners have reviewed and accepted the risk to go live without further testing only then it can be acceptable to end testing.

5.2.4 Test Execution Schedule

Once the various test cases and test procedures are produced and assembled into test suites, the test suites can be arranged in a test execution schedule that defines the order in which they are to be run. The test execution schedule should take into account factors such as prioritization, dependencies, confirmation tests, regression tests, and the most efficient sequence for executing the tests.

Ideally, test cases would be ordered to run based on their **priority levels**, usually by executing the test cases with the highest priority first. However, this practice may not work if the test cases have **dependencies** or the features being tested have dependencies.

For example, if a test case with a higher priority is dependent on a test case with a lower priority, the lower priority test case must be executed first.

Similarly, if there are dependencies across test cases, they must be ordered appropriately regardless of their relative priorities. Confirmation and regression tests must be prioritized as well, based on the importance of rapid feedback on changes, but here again, dependencies may apply.

In some cases, various sequences of tests are possible, with differing levels of efficiency associated with those sequences. In such cases, trade-offs between efficiency of test execution versus adherence to prioritization must be made.

Exercise:

The following diagram shows the logical dependencies between a set of six requirements, where a dependency is shown by an arrow. R3 and R6 are critical requirements having the highest priority for execution. What will be the test execution schedule?

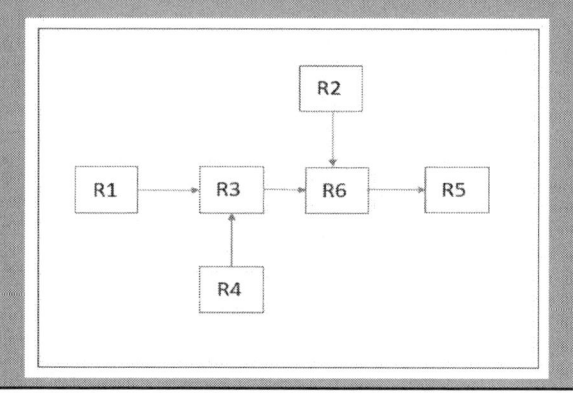

```
                        R2
                        |
                        v
    R1 ---> R3 ---> R6 ---> R5
            ^
            |
            R4
```

R3 and R6 are critical requirement but they have dependencies on other requirements. Hence the execution schedule will be

R1 →R4 →R3 → R2 →R6 →R5 or
R4 →R1 →R3 → R2 →R6 →R5

Test cases are run based on their priority levels, usually by executing the test cases with the highest priority first. However, this practice may not work if the test cases have dependencies or the features being tested have dependencies.

Exercise:

The following table shows the test cases that are used to test a banking system

Test ID	Test case Name	Dependency	Priority
TC1.	Login	None	2
TC2.	Check Balance	TC1	2
TC3.	Check Statement	TC1	3
TC4.	Transfer payment	TC2	1

What will be the test execution schedule based on the priority of test cases?

Though TC4 is having the highest priority it is dependent on TC2 which in turn is dependent on TC1. Hence the order of execution based on priority will be

TC1 → TC2 → TC4 → TC3

5.2.5 Factors Influencing the Test Effort

Test effort estimation involves predicting the amount of test-related work that will be needed in order to meet the objectives of the testing for a particular project, release, or iteration. Following factors may influence the test effort.

Product characteristics

- The risks associated with the product
- The quality of the test basis
- The size of the product
- The complexity of the product domain
- The requirements for quality characteristics (e.g., security, reliability)
- The required level of detail for test documentation
- Requirements for legal and regulatory compliance

Development process characteristics

- The stability and maturity of the organization
- The development model in use
- The test approach
- The tools used
- The test process
- Time pressure

People characteristics

- The skills and experience of the team member on similar projects and products (e.g., domain knowledge)
- Team cohesion and leadership

Test results

- The number and severity of defects found
- The amount of rework required

5.2.6 Test Estimation Techniques

Two approaches for the estimation of test effort are covered in this syllabus:

The metrics-based technique- estimating the test effort based either from previous projects or similar projects or general industry values.

The metrics used for estimation may include:

- Details of project budgets.
- Details of number of test conditions identified.
- Details of number of test cases developed.
- Details of number of test cases executed.
- Details of time taken to develop test cases.
- Details of time taken to execute test cases.
- Details of defects data.
- Details of timeframe to set up the test environment.
- Details of the number of environment outages.

With this approach, it is possible to estimate quite accurately what the cost and time required for a similar project would be.

It is important that the actual costs and time for testing are accurately recorded. These can then be used to revalidate and possibly update the metrics for use on the next similar project.

The expert-based technique- estimating the test effort based on the experience of a person who will be carrying out the relevant testing tasks or by experts. In this context 'experts' could be:

- Business experts
- Technical experts
- Test architects
- Test consultants
- Developers
- Technical architects
- Technical designers

There are many ways that this approach could be used. Here are two examples:

- Ask the task owners to get the estimate of their task in isolation. Amalgamate the individual estimates when received; build in any required contingency, to arrive at the estimate.
- Distribute to known experts who develop their individual view of the overall estimate and then meet together to discuss/debate and agree on the estimate that will go forward.

Expert estimating can use either of the above approaches individually or mix and match them as required.

Examples of estimation techniques in sequential software development:

- **Defect removal models** are examples of the **metrics-based approach**, where volumes of defects and time to remove them are captured and reported, which then provides a basis for estimating future projects of a similar nature.
- **Wideband Delphi estimation technique** is an example of the **expert-based approach** in which a group of experts provides estimates based on their experience.

Examples of estimation techniques in Agile software development:

- **Burndown charts** are examples of the **metrics-based approach** as effort remaining is being captured and reported, and is then used to feed into the team's velocity to determine the amount of work the team can do in the next iteration.
- **Poker planning** is an example of the **expert-based approach**, as team members are estimating the effort to deliver a feature based on their experience.

5.3 Test Monitoring and Control

Test monitoring has the following purpose:

- **Gather information to be monitored** – This is collected manually or automatically using a tool.
- **Provide feedback and visibility** – Comparing the collected information about test activities against the planned. E.g. number of test cases executed vs planned.

Test control describes any guiding or corrective actions taken as a result of information and metrics gathered and (possibly) reported. Actions may cover any test activity and may affect any other software lifecycle activity.

Examples of test control actions include:

- Re-prioritizing tests when an identified risk occurs (e.g. software delivered late)
- Changing the test schedule due to availability or unavailability of a test environment or other resources
- Re-evaluating whether a test item meets an entry or exit criterion due to rework

5.3.1 Metrics used in Testing

Metrics can be collected during and at the end of test activities in order to assess:

- Progress against the planned schedule and budget
- The current quality of the test object
- Adequacy of the test approach
- Effectiveness of the test activities with respect to the objectives

Common test metrics include:

- **Percentage of planned work done** - for test case preparation, test cases implemented, work done in test environment preparation
- **Test case execution** - number of test cases run/not run, test cases passed/failed, and/or test conditions passed/failed
- **Defect information** - defect density, defects found and fixed, failure rate, and confirmation test results
- **Test coverage** - of requirements, user stories, acceptance criteria, risks, or code

- **Task completion** - resource allocation and usage, and effort
- **Cost of testing** - including the cost compared to the benefit of finding the next defect or the cost compared to the benefit of running the next test

5.3.2 Purposes, Contents, and Audiences for Test Reports

The purpose of test reporting is to summarize and communicate test activity information, both during and at the end of a test activity (e.g., a test level).

In general, there are two reports produced during software development lifecycle:

Test progress report - The test report prepared **during a test activity**

During test monitoring and control, the test manager regularly issues test progress reports for stakeholders. In addition to content common to test progress reports and test summary reports, typical test progress reports may also include:

- The status of the test activities and progress against the test plan
- Factors impeding progress
- Testing planned for the next reporting period
- The quality of the test object

Test summary report – The test report prepared at the **end of a test activity**

When the exit criteria are reached, the test manager issues the test summary report. This report provides a summary of the testing performed, based on the latest test progress report and any other relevant information.

Typical test summary reports may include:

- Summary of testing performed
- Information on what occurred during a test period
- Deviations from the plan, including deviations in schedule, duration, or effort of test activities
- Status of testing and product quality with respect to the exit criteria or definition of done
- Factors that have blocked or continue to block progress
- Metrics of defects, test cases, test coverage, activity progress, and resource consumption.
- Residual risks
- Reusable test work products produced

The contents of a test report will vary depending on the following factors:

- **Context of the project** - For example, a complex project with many stakeholders or a regulated project may require more detailed and rigorous reporting than a quick software update.
- **Organizational requirements** - For example, certain organizations have templates for test reports which need to be followed for any given project.
- **Software development lifecycle** - for example, in Agile development, test progress reporting may be incorporated into task boards, defect summaries, and burndown charts, which may be discussed during a daily stand-up meeting.
- **Audience** - The type and amount of information that should be included for a technical audience or a test team may be different from what would be included in an executive summary report. In the first case, detailed information on defect types and trends may be important. In the latter case, a high-level report (e.g., a status summary of defects by priority, budget, schedule, and test conditions passed/failed/not tested) may be more appropriate.

ISO standard (ISO/IEC/IEEE 29119-3) refers to two types of test reports, test progress reports, and test completion reports (called test summary reports in this syllabus) and contains structures and examples for each type.

Key exam take-out

- The **test progress report** is prepared at regular intervals after the entry criteria for testing are reached
- The **test summary report** is prepared after the exit criteria for testing are reached
- The test progress report and test summary report are prepared by **Test Manager.**

5.4 Configuration management

The purpose of configuration management is to establish and maintain the integrity of the products (components, data, and documentation) of the software or system through the project and product life cycle.

During test planning, the configuration management procedures and infrastructure (tools) should be identified and implemented.

The purpose of good configuration management is to:

- Help the testing team to uniquely identify (and to reproduce) the tested item, test documents, the tests, and the test harness.
- Help the organizations know the testware they have, where they are and who owns them.
- Help test teams to make sure they are testing the right version of the code with the appropriate set of related testware.
- Reduce the likelihood that software is changed due to out of date requirements.
- Reduce the likelihood that testers create test suites for requirements that are out of date.
- Help teams know which set of requirements documents and change requests correspond to which software version.
- Establish the relationship between the system and testware through the project and product lifecycle.

To properly support testing, configuration management may involve ensuring the following:

- All the test and testware items are uniquely identified.
- All the test and testware items are version controlled.
- All the test and testware items are tracked for changes.
- All the test and testware items are linked to each other for traceability.
- Every document and software item is referenced unambiguously in test documentation.

> **Key exam take-out**
>
> Configuration management is a single accessible repository to:
> - Get information about configurable items
> - Enable unique identification of items
> - Track the details of changes
> - Facilitate tracking of relationships between items
> - Make sure the project, and test documents and their versions are correctly identified and cross-referenced to one another and linked directly to the latest version of the code and other related development items (test objects).

5.5 Risk and testing

5.5.1 Definition of Risk

A risk can be defined as the possibility of an event in the future which has negative consequences. Risk is measured in terms of the likelihood of the event happening, and its potential impact. In software development, risks are discussed in terms of those affecting an overall project, set up to develop and deliver a product, as well as those affecting the actual product which is developed.

To ensure that the chance of a product failure is minimized, risk management activities provide a disciplined approach to:

- Identifying both project and product risks
- Analyzing and prioritizing risks
- Implementing actions to deal with those risks (risk mitigation).

Risk-based testing adopts all three stages, from a testing perspective.

Identification and analysis of the risks call on the collective knowledge and insight of the project stakeholders, such as the project management team, the development team, the test team, and the business representatives.

Risk mitigation typically focuses on product risk and uses this information in order to guide the test planning, specification, preparation and execution of tests. This can include decisions on:

- The extent of testing to be carried out
- Prioritization of testing
- Test process to be followed
- Test techniques and tools to be employed
- Determination on non-testing activities which could be employed to reduce risk (e.g. providing training).

Throughout testing, risks should be monitored to identify new risks, to determine changes in already established priorities of risk, and to provide feedback about the residual risk by measuring the effectiveness of critical defect removal and contingency plans.

5.5.2 Product and Project Risks

Risk
A factor that could result in future negative consequences

Project Risk
Impact the success of the project

Product Risk
Impact the quality of the product

Project and product risk

Product risk involves the possibility that a work product (e.g., a specification, component, system, or test) may fail to satisfy the legitimate needs of its users and/or stakeholders. Product risks are also called quality risks when they are associated with specific quality characteristics of a product (e.g., functional suitability, reliability, performance efficiency, usability, security, compatibility, maintainability, and portability). Examples of product risks include:

- The software might not perform its intended functions according to the specification
- The software might not perform its intended functions according to user, customer, and/or stakeholder needs
- System architecture may not adequately support some non-functional requirement(s)
- A particular computation may be performed incorrectly in some circumstances
- A loop control structure may be coded incorrectly
- Response-times may be inadequate for a high-performance transaction processing system

- User experience (UX) feedback might not meet product expectations
- Incorrect calculations in reports (a functional risk related to accuracy)
- Slow response to user input (a non-functional risk related to efficiency and response time)
- Difficulty in understanding screens and fields (a non-functional risk related to usability)
- System not able to operate satisfactorily with other systems (a risk related to compatibility)
- System not able to recover from hardware or software failures (a risk related to recoverability)

Project risk involves the possibility of situations that may have a negative effect on a project's ability to achieve its objectives. Examples of project risks include:

- **Project issues:**
    - Delays may occur in delivery, task completion, or satisfaction of exit criteria or definition of done
    - Inaccurate estimates, reallocation of funds to higher priority projects, or general cost-cutting across the organization may result in inadequate funding
    - Late changes may result in substantial re-work

- **Organizational issues:**
    - Skills, training, and staff may not be sufficient
    - Personnel issues may cause conflict and problems
    - Users, business staff, or subject matter experts may not be available due to conflicting business priorities

- **Political issues:**
    - Testers may not communicate their needs and/or the test results adequately
    - Developers and/or testers may fail to follow up on information found in testing and reviews (e.g., not improving development and testing practices)
    - There may be an improper attitude toward, or expectations of, testing (e.g., not appreciating the value of finding defects during testing)

- **Technical issues:**
    - Requirements may not be defined well enough
    - The requirements may not be met, given existing constraints
    - The test environment may not be ready on time
    - Data conversion, migration planning, and their tool support may be late
    - Weaknesses in the development process may impact the consistency or quality of project work products such as design, code, configuration, test data, and test cases
    - Poor defect management and similar problems may result in accumulated defects and other technical debt

- **Supplier issues:**
    - A third party may fail to deliver a necessary product or service or go bankrupt
    - Contractual issues may cause problems to the project

Project risks may affect both development activities and test activities. In some cases, project managers are responsible for handling all project risks, but it is not unusual for test managers to have responsibility for test-related project risks.

Key exam take-out
Product Risk – A risk impacting the quality of the software (after the software is released to the end-users)
Project Risk - A risk which can impact the project success (before the software is released to the end-users)

5.5.3 Risk-based testing and Product Quality

As we have discussed earlier exhaustive testing is not possible therefore a risk-based testing approach is required. These techniques help in deciding the amount of testing that needs to be done to keep the risk to an acceptable level.

Risk can assist a tester in deciding:

- Where and when to start testing and the order to run tests
- Which areas to focus attention on
- Where to apply most of the testing effort

In general, testing is used to reduce the probability of an adverse event occurring, or to reduce the impact of an adverse event. When a defect does occur in the test phases the team have an opportunity to fix the defect (or partially fix to an acceptable workaround) before the software is released to production. Consequently, the risk of software failure is reduced.

Testing is used as a risk mitigation activity, to provide information about identified risks, as well as providing information on residual (unresolved) risks.

A risk-based approach to testing provides proactive opportunities to reduce the levels of product risk. It involves product risk analysis, which includes the identification of product risks and the assessment of each risk's likelihood and impact. The resulting product risk information is used to guide test planning, the specification, preparation and execution of test cases, and test monitoring and control. Analyzing product risks early contributes to the success of a project.

In a risk-based approach, the results of product risk analysis are used to:

- Determine the **test techniques** to be employed
- Determine the **particular levels and types of testing** to be performed (e.g., security testing, accessibility testing)
- Determine the **extent of testing** to be carried out
- **Prioritize testing** (execution order of test cases) in an attempt to find the critical defects as early as possible
- Determine whether any **additional activities** other than testing could be employed to reduce risk (e.g., providing training to business analyst to create better quality requirements)

Risk-based testing requires the collective knowledge and insight of the project stakeholders to carry out product risk analysis. To ensure that the likelihood of a product failure is minimized, risk management activities provide a disciplined approach to:

- **Analyze** the factor which can result in future negative consequences (risks)
- Determine **which risks are important** to deal with
- Implement **actions to mitigate** those risks
- **Make contingency plans** to deal with the risks should they become actual events

These risks are re-evaluated on a regular basis. In addition, testing may identify new risks, help to determine what risks should be mitigated, and lower uncertainty about risks.

> **Exercise:**
>
> For a new system to be developed following are the likelihood of product risk and impact value.
>
> **Risk1**: likelihood of failure = 20%; impact value = $100,000
>
> **Risk2:** likelihood of failure = 10%; impact value = $150,000
>
> **Risk3**: likelihood of failure = 1%; impact value = $500,000
>
> **Risk4:** likelihood of failure = 2%; impact value = $200,000
>
> Which of the above would require more testing to mitigate the risk?

For Risk1, the likelihood × impact value = $20,000

For Risk2 the likelihood × impact value = $15,000

For Risk3 the likelihood × impact value = $5,000

For Risk4 the likelihood × impact value = $4,000

Risk1 is having the highest impact value based on likelihood of failure. Therefore, more testing would be required to mitigate this risk.

5.6 Defects management

Since one of the main objectives of testing is to find defects, the discrepancies between actual and expected outcomes need to be logged.

Defects should be tracked from discovery and classification to correction and confirmation of the solution. This is often facilitated by a **defect management system.**

During the defect management process, some of the reports may turn out to be a false positive and not an actual failure due to a defect. For example, a test may fail when a network connection is broken or times out. This behavior does not result from a defect in the test object, but is an anomaly that needs to be investigated. Testers should attempt to minimize the number of false positives reported as defects.

Defects may be raised during coding, static analysis, reviews, development, or during dynamic testing or in the live environment. They may be raised for issues in code or the working system, or in any type of documentation including development documents, test documents or user information such as "User Manual" or installation guides.

Defect report contains all the information regarding the defect and has the following objectives:

- To provide developers and other stakeholders with feedback about the problem to enable identification, isolation, and correction as necessary
- To provide test managers a means of tracking the quality of the work product and the impact on the testing
- To provide ideas for development and test process improvement

A typical defect report raised during dynamic testing includes:

- **Identifier**- To uniquely identify the defect
- **Title/summary-** Short description of the defect being reported
- **Date** – When the defect was reported
- **Author-** The person who is reporting the defect
- **Test item** – Identification of configuration item e.g. build number
- **Environment** – In which environment defect was detected e.g. TEST, DEV etc.
- **Lifecycle phase** - The development phase in which the defect was observed e.g. development, system testing, etc.

- **Description & Test data**- Step-by-step detail of the defect to enable reproduction and resolution. This can include logs, database dumps screenshots, or recordings (if found during test execution)
- **Expected and actual results** – What was the end results expected and what is actually happening
- **Severity** -Impact of defect
- **Priority** -Urgency/priority to fix
- **Current state** - State of the defect report (e.g., open, deferred, duplicate, waiting to be fixed, awaiting retesting, re-opened, closed)
- **Conclusions** – Any conclusions provided by the author or project team members
- **Recommendations** – Any recommendation provided by the author or project team members
- **Approvals** – Any approvals required for the defect
- **Global issues** -Other areas that may be affected by a change resulting from the defect
- **Change history** - Sequence of actions taken by project team members with respect to the defect to isolate, repair, and confirm it as fixed
- **References** - Details of test case that revealed the problem

When a defect management system is used some of the information is auto-generated based on the system configuration and user profile of the team member who has created the defect report. E.g. name of the author, identifier number, reported date, etc.

ISO standard (ISO/IEC/IEEE 29119-3) provides an example of a sample defect report (which refers to defect reports as incident reports).

Key exam take-out

Some of the key elements of a defect report are:
- **Test data**- to reproduce defects including logs, screenshots, database dumps
- **The severity of defect**- the impact of the defect on the business function and/or test execution.
- **Priority**- will help the developers to know the importance or urgency to fix the defect

Exercise:

Look at the defects report below and identify what important information is missing or incorrect?

Defect Title: customer not able to purchase items		
Author: John	**Date:**	**Defect ID:** 196
Test phase: System	**State:** New	
Severity: Low		
Priority: High		
Defect Summary:		
When some of the customers click on 'Pay now' button from the shopping cart, the wrong screen is displayed. The steps to repeat this defect are: 1. Log on to shopping website with customer id and password 2. Search for items and click add to cart 3. Go to cart and click on "pay now "button 4. Customer is redirected back to the login page. Due to this issue, some of the customers cannot complete the purchase from the online website.		

- As this behavior is observed only for some of the customers, details to the **test data** used is important for the developer to replicate the problem. Syllabus 5.6 - A description of the defect to enable reproduction and resolution, including logs, database dumps, screenshots or recordings.
- The severity of this defect is not correct. As this is having a major impact on business. It should be critical or high (based on the number of users affected)

5.7 Relevant glossary terms and keywords

Glossary term	Definition
Analytical test strategy	A test strategy whereby the test team analyzes the test basis to identify the test conditions to cover.
Configuration management	A discipline applying technical and administrative direction and surveillance to: identify and document the functional and physical characteristics of a configuration item, control changes to those characteristics, record and report change processing and implementation status, and verify compliance with specified requirements.
Configuration item	An aggregation of hardware, software or both, that is designated for configuration management and treated as a single entity in the configuration management process. [ISO 24765]
Consultative test strategy	A test strategy whereby the test team relies on the input of one or more key stakeholders to determine the details of the strategy.
Defect density	The number of defects per unit size of a work product. [ISO 24765]
Defect	An imperfection or deficiency in a work product where it does not meet its requirements or specifications. [ISO 24765]
Defect management	The process of recognizing, recording, classifying, investigating, resolving and disposing of defects.
Defects logging	Recording the details of any defects that occurred, e.g. during testing.
Defect report	Documentation of the occurrence, nature, and status of a defect.
Entry criteria	The set of conditions for officially starting a defined task.
Exit criteria	The set of conditions for officially completing a defined task.
Failure rate	The ratio of the number of failures of a given category to a given unit of measure. [ISO 24765]
Methodical test strategy	A test strategy whereby the test team uses a pre-determined set of test conditions such as a quality standard, a checklist, or a collection of generalized, logical test conditions that may relate to a particular domain, application, or type of testing.

Glossary term	Definition
Model-based test strategy	A test strategy whereby the test team derives testware from models. Examples of models used are reliability growth models, usage models such as operational profiles or behavioral models.
Process-compliant test strategy	A test strategy whereby the test team follows a set of predefined processes, whereby the processes address such items as documentation, the proper identification and use of the test basis and test oracle(s), and the organization of the test team.
Product risk	A risk impacting the quality of a product.
Project risk	A risk that impacts project success.
Regression-averse test strategy	A test strategy whereby the test team applies various techniques to manage the risk of regression such as functional and/or non-functional regression test automation at one or more levels.
Risk	A factor that could result in future negative consequences; usually expressed as impact and likelihood.
Risk-based testing	Testing in which the management, selection, prioritization, and use of testing activities and resources are based on corresponding risk types and risk levels.
Risk level	The qualitative or quantitative measure of a risk defined by impact and likelihood.
Standard-compliant test strategy	A test strategy whereby the test team follows a standard. Standards followed may be valid e.g., for a country (legislation standards), a business domain (domain standards), or internally (organizational standards).
Test approach	The implementation of the test strategy for a specific project.
Test control	The activity that develops and applies corrective actions to get a test project on track when it deviates from what was planned.
Test estimation	An approximation related to various aspects of testing.
Test monitoring	The activity that checks the status of testing activities, identifies any variances from planned or expected, and reports status to stakeholders.
Test level	A specific instantiation of a test process.

Glossary term	Definition
Test plan	Documentation describing the test objectives to be achieved and the means and the schedule for achieving them, organized to coordinate testing activities. [ISO 29119]
Test planning	The activity of establishing or updating a test plan.
Test Procedure	A sequence of test cases in execution order, and any associated actions that may be required to set up the initial preconditions and any wrap up activities post execution. [ISO 29119]
Test progress report	A type of test report produced at regular intervals about the progress of test activities against a baseline, risks, and alternatives requiring a decision.
Test Strategy	Documentation aligned with the test policy that describes the generic requirements for testing and details how to perform testing within an organization. [ISO 29119]
Test summary report	A type of test report produced at completion milestones that provides an evaluation of the corresponding test items against exit criteria.
Tester	A person who performs testing.
Test Manager	The person responsible for project management of testing activities, resources, and evaluation of a test object.

5.8 Quiz

Question 1

Which of the following is the key task for the test manager?

a) Create the detailed test execution schedule
b) Prepare and deliver a test progress report.
c) Review tests prepared by testers.
d) Coordinate with network and other teams for environment setup.

Question 2

Which of the following statement correctly describes the difference between methodical and reactive test strategy for testing?

a) Methodical test strategy is based on the models, whereas reactive test strategy is based on the instructions of the business domain experts.
b) Methodical test strategy implements tests based on external rules and standards, whereas in reactive test strategy tests are implemented based on the prior test results.
c) In methodical test strategy, tests are based on a list of likely failures, whereas in reactive test strategy tests are not pre-planned but are created based on the results of the prior tests.
d) Methodical test strategy uses tests prioritized based on the risk level regression tests, whereas reactive test strategy uses exploratory tests.

Question 3

For an existing online shopping site, new functionality is developed where the user can request a duplicate invoice by email. A tester who is new to the project is testing that functionality.

While testing, the tester has observed that if there are multiple purchase items in the invoice it is causing some minor formatting issues during printing.

Tester has written the defect report to highlight this issue with the following information:

Defect ID: 2156

Title: formatting issue with the invoice

Short summary: All the footer information is not printed for the duplicate invoice having multiple purchase items.

Expected result: All the footer information should be printed for the duplicate invoice.

What is the MOST important information that is missed by the tester in the above defect report?

a) Test data used for testing.
b) The actual test results.
c) Date and author of the defect
d) Severity and priority of the defect.

Question 4

Which of the following are potential drawbacks of independent testing?

1. Independent testers will increase the overall project cost.
2. Developers can lose a sense of responsibility for quality.
3. Independent testers can disprove assumptions made by project stakeholders.
4. Independent testers may not have all the information about the test object.

a) 1 and 2.
b) 1 and 3.
c) 2 and 4.
d) 3 and 4.

Question 5

Which of the following TWO can be considered as the objectives of a good configuration management system?

a) To ensure all the planned test have been executed.
b) To ensure all test items are related to each other.
c) To ensure all the requirements are covered by test cases.
d) To ensure all test items are tracked for changes.

Question 6

Which one of the following is the characteristic of a metrics-based approach for test estimation?

a) Average of estimates collected from developers.
b) Overall estimates collected from test managers.
c) Overall estimate agreed with the testers.
d) Testing budget details from a similar project.

Question 7

Which of the following TWO are examples of product risk?

a) Late changes resulting in a lot of re-work.
b) The requirements may not be met due to existing constrains.
c) Customer not getting the desired user experience from the product.
d) Some of the non-functional requirements are not supported by the system architecture.

Question 8

Which of the following is **NOT** included as a part of test summary report?

a) Reusable test work products produced.
b) Deviations from the test approach.
c) Defining pass/fail criteria.
d) Details of residual risk

5.9 Answers

1	2	3	4	5	6	7	8
B	C	D	C	B, D	D	C, D	C

Question 1

FL-5.1.2 (K1) Identify the tasks of a test manager and tester

Justification

a) Not correct – This is the task of the tester. (Syllabus 5.1.2)
b) **Correct** – This is the task of the test manager. (Syllabus 5.1.2)
c) Not correct – This is the task of the tester. (Syllabus 5.1.2)
d) Not correct – This is the task of the tester. (Syllabus 5.1.2)

Question 2

FL-5.2.2 (K2) Differentiate between various test strategies

Justification

a) Not correct – This describes the model and consultative, not the methodical and reactive test strategy. (Syllabus 5.2.2)
b) Not correct – This describes the process-compliant, not the methodical test strategy. (Syllabus 5.2.2)
c) **Correct** – Methodical test strategy uses taxonomy of likely failures to plan the tests while in reactive test strategy tests are not pre-planned but created based on the previous test results test. (Syllabus 5.2.2)
d) Not correct – It is the analytical test strategy which tests which are prioritized based on the level of risk and not the methodical test strategy. (Syllabus 5.2.2)

Question 3

FL-5.6.1 (K3) Write a defect report, covering defects found during testing.

Justification

a) Not correct – This is not important as the behavior is similar for all the invoices.
b) Not correct – This is not important as the details are already in the summary.
c) Not correct – This information is missing but is not so important for this situation.
d) **Correct** – This is an important piece of information which is required from the tester. Looking closely at the situation, as it is a minor formatting problem, this issue is having low severity and low priority to fix. This need to be communicated to the developers to help them decide which defect to fix first. (Syllabus 5.6)

Question 4

FL-5.1.1 (K2) Explain the benefits and drawbacks of independent testing

Justification

1. This is not correct. There is more chance that independent testers will find more defects and decrease the project cost.
2. This is correct. When the developers are aware that there is some independent testing after they have tested their own code, they may lose a sense of responsibility for quality.
3. This is not a drawback but a potential benefit that the independent testers can verify, challenge, or disprove assumptions made by stakeholders during the specification and implementation of the system. (Syllabus 5.1.1)
4. This is correct. This is a potential drawback that the independent testers may not have all the information about the test object. (Syllabus 5.1.1)

Thus:

a) Not correct
b) Not correct
c) **Correct**
d) Not correct

Question 5

FL-5.4.1 (K2) Summarize how configuration management supports testing

Justification

a) Not correct – Ensuring that all the planned test is executed is not the objective of the configuration management system.
b) **Correct** – This is one of the objectives of a good configuration management system. (Syllabus 5.4)
c) Not correct – Coverage of the requirements is not the objective of the configuration management system.
d) **Correct** – This is one of the objectives of a good configuration management system. (Syllabus 5.4)

Question 6

FL-5.2.6 (K2) Explain the difference between two estimation techniques: the metrics-based technique and the expert-based technique

Justification

a) Not correct – This is characteristic of the expert-based approach where the estimation of the tasks is based on the estimates from the owners of the tasks or by experts. (Syllabus 5.2.6)
b) Not correct – This is characteristic of the expert-based approach where the estimation of the tasks is based on the estimates from the owners of the tasks or by experts. (Syllabus 5.2.6)
c) Not correct – This is characteristic of the expert-based approach where the estimation of the tasks is based on the estimates from the owners of the tasks or by experts. (Syllabus 5.2.6)
d) **Correct** – This is characteristic of metrics-based approach where the estimation of the test effort is based on metrics of similar projects in the past, or based on typical values. (Syllabus 5.2.6)

Question 7

FL-5.5.2 (K2) Distinguish between project and product risks

Justification

a) Not correct – This is a project risk, not a product risk (Syllabus 5.3.2)
b) Not correct – This is a project risk, not a product risk (Syllabus 5.3.2)
c) **Correct** – This is a product risk. (Syllabus 5.3.2)
d) **Correct** – This is a product risk. (Syllabus 5.3.2)

Question 8

FL-5.3.2 (K2) Summarize the purposes, content, and audiences for test reports

Justification

a) Not correct – This information is included in the test summary report (Syllabus 5.3.2)
b) Not correct – This information is included in the test summary report (Syllabus 5.3.2)
c) **Correct** – This information is defined earlier in the test project during planning.
d) Not correct – This information is included in the test summary report (Syllabus 5.3.2)

6 Tool Support for Testing

Learning objectives for Tool support	218
6.1 Test Tool Consideration	219
6.1.1 Test tool classification	219
6.1.2 Benefits and Risks of Test Automation	225
6.1.3 Special considerations for Test Execution and Test Management Tools	226
6.2 Effective Use of Tools	228
6.2.1 Main Principles for Tool Selection	228
6.2.2 Pilot Projects for Introducing a Tool into an Organization	229
6.2.3 Success Factors for Tools	229
6.3 Relevant glossary terms and keywords	230
6.4 Quiz	233
6.5 Answers	236

Learning objectives for Test Tool

Following learning objectives are covered in this chapter:

6.1 Test tool considerations

FL-6.1.1 (K2) Classify test tools according to their purpose and the test activities they support

FL-6.1.2 (K1) Identify benefits and risks of test automation

FL-6.1.3 (K1) Remember special considerations for test execution and test management tools

6.2 Effective use of tools

FL-6.2.1 (K1) Identify the main principles for selecting a tool

FL-6.2.2 (K1) Recall the objectives for using pilot projects to introduce tools

FL-6.2.3 (K1) Identify the success factors for evaluation, implementation, deployment, and on-going support of test tools in an organization

6.1 Test Tool Consideration

Test tools can be used to support one or more testing activities. Such tools include:

- Tools that are directly used in testing, such as test execution tools and test data preparation tools
- Tools that are used for reporting and monitoring test execution, and managing requirements, test cases, test procedures, automated test scripts, test results, test data, and defects.
- Tools that are used for analysis and evaluation
- Tools that assist in testing e.g. a spreadsheet is also a test tool if it used to support any of the test activity.

6.1.1 Test tool classification

There are a number of tools that support different aspects of testing. Tools are classified according to the testing activities that they support. Some tools may support more than one activity but are classified under the activity with which they are most closely associated. Some commercial tools offer support for only one type of activity; other commercial tool vendors offer suites or families of tools that may provide support for many or all of these activities.

Testing tools can contribute to testing in a number of ways, they can:

- Improve the efficiency of test activities by automating repetitive tasks or tasks that require significant resources when done manually (e.g., test execution, regression testing)
- Improve the efficiency of test activities by supporting manual test activities throughout the test process
- Improve the quality of test activities by allowing for more consistent testing and a higher level of defect reproducibility
- Enable the automation of activities that could not be executed manually such as large-scale performance testing of client-server applications.
- Increase reliability of testing. For example, by automating large data comparisons or simulating behavior.

Some types of test tools can be **intrusive**. This means that the tool itself can affect the actual outcome of the test. For example, a performance testing tool may insert extra lines to code to mimic the user delay. This may affect the actual response time of an application. Another example can be of a code coverage tool that adds extra statements into the code. When the code is executed the extra statements inserted write back to a log to identify which statements and branches have been executed.

The consequence of using intrusive tools is called the **probe effect** and testers need to be aware of this to try to keep its impact to a minimum.

Some tools offer support more appropriate for developers (e.g., tool that are used during component and integration testing). Such tools are marked with "(D)" in the classifications which follow.

Tool support for management of testing and testware

Management tools apply to any test activities over the entire software life cycle. Examples of tools that support management of testing and testware include:

Test management tools & application lifecycle management tools (ALM)

Characteristics of these tools include:

- Support for the management of tests and the scheduling of different testing activities
- Interfaces to test execution tools, defect tracking tools and requirement management tools
- Independent version control or interface with an external configuration management tool
- Support for traceability of tests, test results and defects to source documents, such as requirement specifications
- Logging of test results and generation of progress reports
- Quantitative analysis (metrics) related to the tests (e.g., tests run, tests passed) and the test object (e.g., defects raised)
- Apply metrics to provide information about the test object, and to control and improve the test process

Requirements management tools

Characteristics of these tools include:

- Store requirement statements, check for consistency and undefined (missing) requirements.
- Allow requirements to be prioritized and enable individual tests to be traceable to requirements, functions and/or features.
- Report traceability, coverage of requirements in progress reports.

Defects management tools (defect tracking tools)

Characteristics of these tools include:

- Facilitate the prioritization of defects.
- Allow defect assignment to different team members for actions required (e.g., developer to fix or to tester for confirmation test).
- Attribution of status (e.g. rejected, ready to be tested or deferred to next release).
- Store and manage defects.
- Provide support for statistical analysis and creation of defect reports.

Configuration management tools

Configuration management (CM) tools are not strictly testing tools but are typically used to store information about versions and builds of the software and testware, traceability between software and testware, release management, baselining, and access control. They are particularly useful when developing and testing more than one configuration of the hardware/software (e.g. for different operating system versions, different libraries, different browsers, or a different set of computers).

Characteristics of these tools include:

- Store information about versions and builds of software and testware.
- Enable traceability between testware, software work products and product variants.

Continuous integration tools (D)

Continuous Integration (CI) tools are not strictly testing tools, they help multiple developers to make changes to the shared code repository and integrate all the changed components regularly. This makes it easier for users to obtain a fresh build. Characteristics of these tools include:

- Allows regular code changes into a shared code repository
- Earlier detection of integration problems and conflicting changes
- Provides frequent feedback to the development team on whether the code is working

Tool support for static testing

Static testing tools are associated with the activities and benefits described in chapter 3.

Static analysis tools (D)

Static analysis tools support developers and testers in finding defects before dynamic testing. Characteristics of these tools include:

- The enforcement of coding standards
- The analysis of structures and dependencies (e.g. linked web pages)
- Aiding in understanding the code.
- Calculate metrics from the code (e.g. complexity) (input for planning or risk analysis)

Static analysis tools can also be used for review of work products. Some of the simplest static review tools search the requirement document for "weak phrases" that can cause uncertainty and leave room for multiple interpretations. Use of phrases such as "adequate" and "as appropriate" indicates that what is required is either defined elsewhere or, worse, that the requirement is open to subjective interpretation. Phrases such as "but not limited to" and "as a minimum" provide a basis for expanding a requirement or adding future requirements.

Reports produced by the tool with the total number of weak phrases found in a document is an indication of the extent that the specification is ambiguous and incomplete.

Tool support for test design and implementation

Model-based testing tools

Model-based tools are able to validate models of the software. The major benefit of modelling tools is the cost-effectiveness of finding defects in the early stages of development process. Characteristics of these tools include:

- Find defects and inconsistencies in the data or database model
- Find defects in a state model or an object model
- Generate high-level test cases based on the model

Test data preparation tools

Characteristics of these tools include:

- Analyze the requirements document or source code to determine the data required during testing to achieve a level of coverage.
- Take a data set from a production system and "scrub" or "anonymize" it to remove any personal information while still maintaining the internal integrity of that data. The scrubbed data can then be used for testing without the risk of a security leak or misuse of personal information. This is particularly important where large volumes of realistic data are required.
- Generate test data from given sets of input parameters (i.e., for use in random testing). Some of these tools can analyze the database structure to determine what inputs will be required from the testers.

Tool support for test execution and logging

Test execution tools

Characteristics of these tools include:

- Enabling tests to be executed automatically, or semi-automatically, using stored inputs and expected outcomes, through the use of a scripting language.
- Ability to manipulate the tests with limited effort. For example, to repeat the test with different data or to test a different part of the system with similar steps.
- Include dynamic comparison features and provide a test log for each test run.

These tools can also be used to record tests, when they may be referred to as capture playback tools. Capturing test inputs during exploratory testing or unscripted testing can be useful in order to reproduce and/or document a test when a failure occurs.

Coverage tools (D)

Characteristics of these tools include:

- Measure the percentage of specific types of code structure that have been exercised (e.g. statements, decisions, or function calls).
- These tools show how thoroughly the measured type of structure has been exercised by a set of tests.

Test harness (D)

The test harness is often used by developers for unit testing of the components during the development phase. It provides a simulated environment with stubs and drivers for the execution of the unit test cases. Test harness is often required because other components of that environment are not yet ready or to provide a predictable and controllable environment in which the faults can be localized.

Tool support for Performance measurement and dynamic analysis

Performance measurement and dynamic analysis tools are essential in supporting performance and load testing activities, as these activities cannot effectively be done manually.

Performance testing tools

These tools are used to assess system performance. Characteristics of these tools include:

- Simulate a load on an application, or a database, or a network or server.
- Monitor and report on how a system behaves under a variety of simulated usage conditions.

Dynamic analysis tools (D)

They are typically used in component and component integration testing, and when testing middleware. Characteristics of these tools include:

- Find defects that are evident only when the software is executing. E.g. memory leaks.

Tool support for specialized testing needs

In addition to tools that support the general test process, there are many other tools that support more specific testing for non-functional characteristics.

6.1.2 Benefits and Risks of Test Automation

Simply purchasing or leasing a tool does not guarantee success. Each type of new tool may require additional effort to achieve real and lasting benefits. There are potential benefits and opportunities with the use of tools in testing, but there are also risks. This is particularly true of test execution tools (which is often referred to as test automation).

Potential benefits of using tools to support test execution include:

- Repetitive work is reduced (e.g. running regression tests, re-entering the same test data, and checking against coding standards), thus time is saved.
- Greater consistency and repeatability (e.g. tests executed by a tool in the same order with the same frequency, tests are consistently derived from requirements, and test data is created coherently)
- Objective assessment (e.g. static measures, coverage, and system behavior)
- Ease of access to information about tests or testing (e.g. statistics and graphs about test progress, defects rates, and performance).

Risks of using tools to support testing include:

- Unrealistic expectations for the tool (including functionality and ease of use)
- Under-estimating the time, cost and effort for the initial introduction of a tool (including training and external expertise)
- Under-estimating the time and effort needed to achieve significant and continuing benefits from the tool (including the need for changes in the testing process and continuous improvement of the way the tool is used)
- Under-estimating the effort required to maintain the test work products generated by the tool
- Over-reliance on the tool (replacement for test design or where manual testing would be better)
- Version control of test work products may be neglected
- Relationships and interoperability issues between critical tools may be neglected, such as requirements management tools, configuration management tools, defect management tools and tools from multiple vendors
- Tool vendor may go out of business, retire the tool, or sell the tool to a different vendor

- Poor response for support, upgrades, and defect fixes from the tool vendor
- An open-source project may be suspended
- Tool may not work partially or completely on a new platform or technology
- Lack of ownership of the tool (e.g., for mentoring, updates, etc.)

6.1.3 Special considerations for Test Execution and Test Management Tools

Test execution tools

Test execution tools execute test objects using automated test scripts. This type of tool often requires significant effort in order to achieve significant benefits.

Capturing test approach create the automated test scripts by recording the actions of a manual tester with specific data and actions as part of each script. This type of script may be unstable when unexpected events occur. Therefore, these automated scripts require ongoing maintenance as the system's user interface evolves over time.

Data-driven approach separates out the test inputs (the data) and expected results, usually into a spreadsheet, and uses a more generic script that can read the test data and perform the same test with different data.

keyword-driven test approach In this approach, the spreadsheet contains keywords describing the actions to be taken (also called action words), and test data. These Keywords are mostly, used to represent high-level business interactions with a system (e.g., "cancel order"). Each keyword is typically used to represent a number of detailed interactions between an actor and the system under test. Sequences of keywords (including relevant test data) are used to specify test cases. A keyword may be implemented as one or more executable test scripts.

Tool reads test cases written as a sequence of keywords and call the appropriate test scripts which implement the keyword functionality. The scripts are implemented in a highly modular manner to enable easy mapping to specific keywords. The primary advantages of keyword-driven test automation are:

- Keywords that relate to a particular application or business domain can be defined by domain experts. This can make the task of test case specification more efficient.
- A person with primarily domain expertise can benefit from automatic test case execution (once the keywords have been implemented as scripts) without having to understand the underlying automation code.

- Test cases written using keywords are easier to maintain because they are less likely to need modification if details in the software under test change.
- Test case specifications are independent of their implementation. The keywords can be implemented using a variety of scripting languages and tools.
- Testers (even if they are not familiar with the scripting language) can then define tests using the keywords and associated data, which can be tailored to the application being tested.

Technical expertise in the scripting language is needed for all approaches (either by testers or by specialists in test automation). However, testers who are not familiar with the scripting language can also contribute by creating test data and/or keywords for these predefined scripts.

Regardless of the scripting technique used, the actual results for each test need to be compared to expected results from the test. This can be done either dynamically while the test is running or post-execution when the actual results are stored for later comparison.

Model-Based Testing (MBT) tools enable a functional specification to be captured in the form of a model, such as an activity diagram. This task is generally performed by a system designer. The MBT tool interprets the model in order to create test case specifications which can then be saved in a test management tool and/or executed by a test execution tool.

Test management tools

Test management tools need to interface with other tools or spreadsheets for various reasons including:

- To produce useful information in a format that fits the needs of the organization
- To maintain consistent traceability to requirements in a requirements management tool
- To link with test object version information in the configuration management tool

This is particularly important to consider when using an integrated tool. For example, Application Lifecycle Management which includes a separate module for requirement management, test management, defect management, project schedule, and budget information. These modules are used independently by different groups within an organization.

6.2 Effective Use of Tools

6.2.1 Main Principles for Tool Selection

The main principles of introducing a tool into an organization include:

- Assessment of the maturity of the organization, its strengths, and weaknesses
- Identification of opportunities for an improved test process supported by tools
- Understanding the technologies used by the test object(s), in order to select a tool that is compatible with that technology
- Understanding the build and continuous integration tools already in use within the organization, in order to ensure tool compatibility and integration
- Evaluation of the tool against clear requirements and objective criteria
- Consideration of whether or not the tool is available for a free trial period (and for how long)
- Evaluation of the vendor (including training, support and commercial aspects) or support for non- commercial (e.g., open-source) tools
- Identification of internal requirements for coaching and mentoring in the use of the tool
- Evaluation of training needs, considering the testing (and test automation) skills of those who will be working directly with the tool(s)
- Consideration of the pros and cons of various licensing models (e.g., commercial or open-source)
- Estimation of a cost-benefit ratio based on a concrete business case (if required)

As a final step, a proof-of-concept evaluation should be done to establish whether the tool performs effectively with the software under test and within the current infrastructure or, if necessary, to identify changes needed to that infrastructure to use the tool effectively.

6.2.2 Pilot Projects for Introducing a Tool into an Organization

The pilot project for introducing tool into an organization starts after the tool selection is completed and the Proof-of-Concept (POC) is successful. Experience shows that the following are important objectives in running a successful pilot project:

- To gain **in-depth knowledge** about the tool. This includes understanding both the strength and weaknesses of the tool.
- To evaluate how the tool **fits with existing processes and practices**. It will help in determining what would need to change in existing processes and practices to accommodate the tool.
- To decide on standard ways of **using, managing, storing, and maintaining** the tool and the test work products. This will include deciding on naming conventions for files and tests, selecting coding standards, creating libraries and defining the modularity of test suites.
- To assess whether the benefits will be achieved at a **reasonable cost**.
- To understand the **metrics** that the organization wish the tool to collect and report. The tool should be then configured to ensure these metrics can be captured and reported.

6.2.3 Success Factors for Tools

Success factors for the evaluation, implementation, deployment and on-going support of the tool within an organization include:

- **Incrementally** rolling out the tool to the rest of the organization
- **Adapting and improving processes** to fit with the use of the tool
- Providing **training and coaching/mentoring** for new users.
- Defining **usage guidelines** (i.e. defining internal standards for automation)
- Implementing a way to **gather usage information** from the actual use of the tool
- **Monitoring** tool use and benefits.
- **Providing support** to the users of a given tool
- Gathering **lessons learned** from all users

6.3 Relevant glossary terms and keywords

Glossary term	Definition
Configuration management tool	A tool that supports configuration management activities. Configuration management is a discipline applying technical and administrative direction and surveillance to identify and document the functional and physical characteristics of a configuration item, control changes to those characteristics, record and report change processing and implementation status, and verify that it complies with specified requirements.
Coverage tool / Coverage measurement tool	A tool that provides objective measures of what structural elements, e.g. statements, branches have been exercised by a test suite.
Data-Driven testing	A scripting technique that uses data files to contain the test data and expected results needed to execute the test scripts.
Debugging tool	A tool used by programmers to reproduce failures, investigate the state of programs and find the corresponding defect. Debuggers enable programmers to execute programs step by step, to halt a program at any program statement and to set and examine program variables.
Dynamic analysis tool	A tool that evaluates a component or system based on its behavior during execution. These tools are most commonly used to identify unassigned pointers, check pointer arithmetic and to monitor the allocation, use and de-allocation of memory and to flag memory leaks.
Defects / Defect management tool	A tool that facilitates the process of recognizing, recording, classifying, investigating, resolving, and disposing of defects. They often have workflow-oriented facilities to track and control the allocation, correction and re-testing of defects and provide reporting facilities.
Keyword-driven testing	A scripting technique in which test scripts contain high-level keywords and supporting files that contain low-level scripts that implement those keywords.
Load testing tool	A tool that supports a type of performance testing conducted to evaluate the behavior of a component or system under varying loads, usually between anticipated conditions of low, typical, and peak usage

Glossary term	Definition
Modelling tool	A tool that supports the validation of models of the software or system.
Monitoring tool	A software tool or hardware device that runs concurrently with the component or system under test and supervises, records and/or analyzes the behavior of the component or system. [ISO 24765]
Probe effect	An unintended change in the behavior of a component or system caused by measuring it. For example, performance may be slightly worse when performance testing tools are being used.
Requirements management tool	A tool that supports the recording of requirements, requirements attributes (e.g. priority, knowledge responsible) and annotation, and facilitates traceability through layers of requirements and requirements change management. Some requirements management tools also provide facilities for static analysis, such as consistency checking and violations to pre-defined requirements rules.
Review tools / review process support tool	A tool that provides support to the review process. Typical features include review planning and tracking support, communication support, collaborative reviews and a repository for collecting and reporting of metrics.
Security tool	A tool that supports attributes of software products that bear on its ability to prevent unauthorized access, whether accidental or deliberate, to programs and data.
Static analysis tool	A tool that carries out static analysis. Static analysis is the process of evaluating a component or system without executing it, based on its form, structure, content, or documentation.
Stress testing tool	A tool that supports testing conducted to evaluate a system or component at or beyond the limits of its anticipated or specified workloads, or with reduced availability of resources such as access to memory or servers.
Test Automation	The use of software to perform or support test activities, e.g., test management, test design, test execution and results checking.

Glossary term	Definition
Test comparator	A test tool to perform automated test comparison. Test comparison is the process of identifying differences between the actual results produced by the component or system under test and the expected results for a test. Test comparison can be performed during test execution (dynamic comparison) or after test execution.
Test data preparation tool	A type of test tool that enables data to be selected from existing databases or created, generated, manipulated and edited for use in testing.
Test design tool	A tool that supports the test design activity by generating test inputs from a specification that may be held in a CASE tool repository, e.g. requirements management tool, or from specified test conditions held in the tool itself.
Test harness	A test environment comprised of stubs and drivers needed to execute a test suite.
Test execution tool	A test tool that executes tests against a designated test item and evaluates the outcomes against expected results and postconditions.
Test management tool	A tool that supports test management. It often has several capabilities, such as testware management, scheduling of tests, the logging of results, progress tracking, defects management and test reporting.
Test oracle	A source to determine expected results to compare with the actual result of the software under test. An oracle may be the existing system (for a benchmark), a user manual, or an individual's specialized knowledge, but should not be the code.

6.4 Quiz

Question 1

Which of the following test tools (1-4) are characterized by the classification (A-D) below?

1. Test data preparation tools.
2. Requirement management tools.
3. Test harness tools.
4. Dynamic analysis tools.

A. Management of testing and testware.
B. Test design and implementation.
C. Performance measurement and dynamic analysis.
D. Test execution and logging.

a) 1D, 2A, 3B, 4C.
b) 1B, 2A, 3D, 4C.
c) 1B, 2C, 3D, 4A.
d) 1A, 2B, 3D, 4C.

Question 2

The tools that support specific testing for non-functional characteristics belong to which classification of tool support?

a) Management of testing and testware.
b) Test design and implementation.
c) Specialized testing needs.
d) Performance measurement and dynamic analysis.

Question 3

Which of the following is a characteristic of a static analysis tool?

a) Store information about versions and builds of software.
b) Allow regular code changes into the shared code repository.
c) Calculate the complexity of code.
d) Creates stubs and drivers for testing.

Question 4

Match each of the following tools (1-4) to its MOST suitable activity (A-D):

1. Requirements management tools
2. Dynamic analysis tools
3. Continuous integration tools
4. Test harness

A. Finding memory leaks
B. Simulating the environment
C. Prevent integration problems
D. Traceability to test objects

a) 1D, 2A, 3C, 4B.
b) 1B, 2A, 3D, 4C.
c) 1D, 2C, 3B, 4A.
d) 1D, 2C 3A, 4B.

Question 5

Which of the following is a MOST likely benefit of using a test management tool?

a) It is easy to maintain all the requirements.
b) It is easy to track defects.
c) It is easy to maintain different versions of test assets.
d) It is easy to provide real time metrics related to the tests.

Question 6

Which of the following is MOST likely to be considered when selecting a new tool for an organization?

a) Release cycle of the organization.
b) The current quality of the test object.
c) The technologies used by the test object.
d) The defect density of the projects where the tool can be used.

Question 7

Which of the following would NOT be helpful for successfully implementing a new tool for an organization?

a) Gathering lessons learned from all the users
b) Roll out the tool to as many users as possible within the organization to see benefits.
c) Evaluate the tool features against clear requirements and objective criteria
d) Training required for the tool users.

6.5 Answers

1	2	3	4	5	6	7
B	C	C	A	D	C	B

Question 1

FL-6.1.1 (K2) Classify test tools according to their purpose and the test activities they support

Justification

- Test data preparation tools are an example of test design and implementation tools: Syllabus 6.1.1, Tools that support design and implementation. (1B)
- Requirement management tools are an example of tools for management of testing and testware: Syllabus 6.1.1, Tools that support management of testing and testware. (2A)
- Test harness tools are an example of test execution and logging: Syllabus 6.1.1, Tools that support test execution and logging. (3D)
- Dynamic analysis tools are examples of performance measurement and dynamic analysis: Syllabus 6.1.1, Tools that support performance measurement and dynamic analysis. (4C)

Thus:

a) Not correct
b) **Correct**
c) Not correct
d) Not correct

Question 2

FL-6.1.1 (K2) Classify test tools according to their purpose and the test activities they support

Justification

Specialized testing tools support specific testing for non-functional characteristics. Examples of these tools are:

o   Data quality assessment tools
o   Data conversion and migration tools
o   Usability testing tools
o   Accessibility testing tools
o   Localization testing tools
o   Security testing tools
o   Portability testing tools

Thus:

a) Not correct
b) Not correct
c) **Correct**
d) Not correct

Question 3

FL-6.1.1 (K2) Classify test tools according to their purpose and the test activities they support

Justification

a) Not correct – This is the characteristic of configuration management tool.
b) Not correct – This is the characteristic of continuous integration tool.
c) **Correct** – Static Analysis tool calculate the complexity of code based on the number of decisions and some other factors.
d) Not correct – This is the characteristic of Test harness tool.

Question 4

FL-6.1.1 (K2) Classify test tools according to their purpose and the test activities they support

Justification

- Requirements management tools provide traceability to test objects. Syllabus 6.1.1 (1D)
- Dynamic analysis finds memory leaks in the system. Syllabus 6.1.1 (2A)
- Continuous integration tools allow regularly integrating code changes into a shared code repository and prevent integration problem when multiple developers are working on code base. Syllabus 6. 1.1 (3C)
- Test harness simulates the environment in which the test object can be run. This is required as other components of that environment are still not available. Syllabus 6.1.1 (4B)

Thus:

a) **Correct**
b) Not correct
c) Not correct
d) Not correct

Question 5

FL-6.1.1 (K2) Classify test tools according to their purpose and the test activities they support

Justification

a) Not correct – This is the main characteristic of requirement management tool. Most of the Test management tools are able to maintain the requirements but this is not the MOST likely benefit.
b) Not correct – This is the main characteristic of defect management tool. Most of the Test management tools are able to maintain defect information but this is not the MOST likely benefit.
c) Not correct – This is the main characteristic of the configuration tool. Most of the Test management tools are able to maintain the version control but this is not the MOST likely benefit.
d) **Correct**– This is the MOST likely benefit of the test management tool to get the metrics related to the tests (e.g. tests run, and tests passed) and the test object (e.g. defects raised), This metrics is used to provide information about the test object.

Question 6

FL-6.2.1 (K1) Identify the main principles for selecting a tool

Justification

a) Not correct – Release cycle of the organization will not affect the new tool selection.
b) Not correct – Current quality of the test object is not considered for a new tool selection.
c) **Correct** – Understanding the technologies used by test object is considered for a new tool selection as the new tool should be compatible with that technology. (Syllabus 6.2.1)
d) Not correct – Defect density of the projects where the tool is used will not affect the tool selection.

Question 7

FL-6.2.1 (K1) Identify the main principles for selecting a tool

Justification

a) Not correct – This would be helpful in successfully implementing a new tool for an organization.
b) **Correct** – This is NOT helpful in successfully implementing a new tool for an organization. The tool should be incrementally rolled out in the organization.
c) Not correct – This would be helpful in successfully implementing a new tool for an organization.
d) Not correct – This would be helpful in successfully implementing a new tool for an organization.

Made in the USA
Columbia, SC
12 July 2021